Henry Warner Slocum

Lawn Tennis in our Own Country

Henry Warner Slocum

Lawn Tennis in our Own Country

ISBN/EAN: 9783337427962

Printed in Europe, USA, Canada, Australia, Japan

Cover: Foto ©Suzi / pixelio.de

More available books at **www.hansebooks.com**

LAWN TENNIS

IN

OUR OWN COUNTRY

BY

H. W. SLOCUM JR.

———— ——

PUBLISHED BY

A. G. SPALDING & BROS.

NEW YORK - PHILADELPHIA - CHICAGO

CONTENTS.

PART I.

THE GAME AS IT *IS* PLAYED.

PART II.

THE GAME AS IT *HAS BEEN* PLAYED.

APPENDIX.

PART I.

THE GAME AS IT *IS* PLAYED.

CHAPTER I.

THE COURT AND EQUIPMENTS OF THE GAME.

"But this the tennis court keeper knows better than I."
—*King Henry IV*.

WHEN Lawn Tennis was first played in England, some years before its introduction in this country, it differed from the game of to-day mainly in the dimensions of the court and net, and the shape or construction of the implements used in playing. If we are to believe what we read, it was the crude invention of an English officer, who, in all probability, was seeking for a game which would not only satisfy the English love of manly sport, but also afford an easy medium of exercise for himself and one or two of his friends. If we had no knowledge on the point we should be quite safe in assuming that the idea was in part suggested by the simple game of Battledore and Shuttlecock, for under the rules formulated by Major Wingfield, Lawn Tennis was played over a net many feet higher than those in use at the present

time, and as, in addition, the lightest and crudest
kind of a racket and balls were used, the contestants
must have been sufficiently elated when they succeeded in striking the ball fairly and raising it over
the many feet of net, without devoting much thought
as to the point of the hostile court in which it should
fall, or, in other words, without any idea of "placing"
the ball, which is so prominent a feature of the
present game. Indeed, it is difficult to conceive how
it would be possible to "place" the ball over a net
five or six feet high, being given a court of the present
dimensions, and yet we read that the court of those
days was even smaller; so that while we may be
under obligations to Major Wingfield for the idea,
we are indebted only to the genius of the times and
a sport-loving generation for the evolution and perfection of the idea, the modern and beautiful game
with its low net, swift and scientific strokes and accurate "placing." No game has developed or improved more than Lawn Tennis during the past few
years, and that fact is an almost unerring indication
that the game has come to stay. I can recall no great
and popular pastime of modern days, except Cricket,
which has not been materially changed for the better
within the last decade or two. Baseball and the
Rugby game of Football, as now played by our
colleges, are notable instances of this proposition.
The most substantial proof of the real merit of these
two games lies in the fact that there was so much in
them to be brought out in recent years, and some of
us might be inclined to differ from the judgment of an
Englishman or an American admirer of Cricket, who
would aver that the only reason why that game has
not changed, is because it was perfect in its beginning.

Any changes in Lawn Tennis, which the future may bring about, will probably be changes in the game itself and not in the court, upon which, or the implements with which, the game is played. There is every reason to believe that a court of 78 feet in length and 27 feet in width, and a net 3 feet high, present the best combination possible to induce speedy play and accurate placing. The first of the Laws of Lawn Tennis, as adopted by the United States National Lawn Tennis Association, specifies the dimensions of the court and height of the net as follows:

THE COURT.

1. **The Court** is 78 feet long, and 27 feet wide. It is divided across the middle by a net, the ends of which are attached to two posts, **A** and **B**, standing 3 feet outside the court on either side. The height of the net is 3 feet

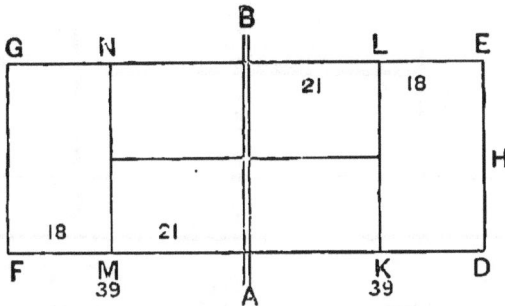

6 inches at the posts, and 3 feet in the middle. At each end of the court, parallel with the net, and 39 feet from it, are drawn the base lines **DE** and **FG**, the ends of which are connected by the side-lines **DF** and **EG**. Half-way between the side-lines, and parallel with them, is drawn the half court line **IH**, dividing the space on each side of the net into two equal parts, the right and left courts. On each

side of the net, at a distance of 21 feet from it, and parallel with it, are drawn the service lines **KL** and **MN**.

The above diagram shows the court when it is to be used for the Single or Single-handed game. When three or four persons are to play, the game being then called the Double or Four-handed game, additional space is added to each side of the court as it is used in the Single-handed game, but the base line remains at the same distance from the net and the service court is the same in every dimension. The following diagram shows the court for

THE THREE-HANDED AND FOUR-HANDED GAMES

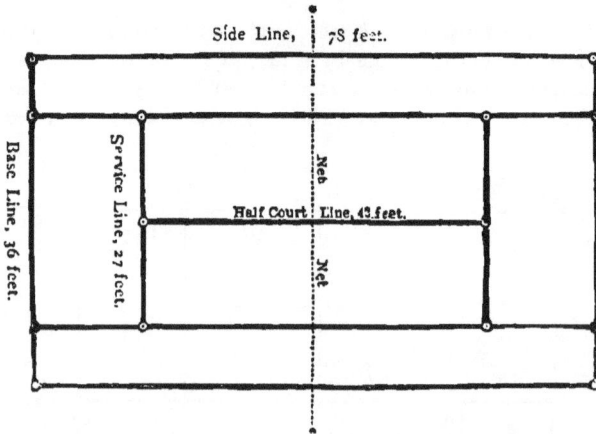

The only difference, therefore, between the Single and Double courts, is a difference in width, both being parallelograms, the former 78 feet in length, and 27 feet in width, and the latter 78 feet in length and 36 feet in width.

When a Lawn Tennis Club is first organized, the question as to whether turf or earth courts shall be

constructed, often causes much discussion. It is a
matter of some consideration, for a Club, inasmuch
as it frequently happens that its membership is
largely influenced by the kind of court which is
adopted. A great number of the most expert
players object to practice on earth courts, on the
ground that such practice injures their play on turf,
and it is well known that a majority of the great
tournaments, which are so pleasant a feature of the
game, are contested on turf. Then again, one who
is to construct a court for private use, will often
hesitate in his selection on account of a lack of
knowledge as to the relative cost, expense of maintaining, durability, etc., of the turf and earth courts.
If I were compelled to choose for myself, and there
were no unusual circumstances to influence my
decision, I should unhesitatingly choose a turf
court. It is probable, however, that there are always
certain conditions, peculiar to any particular Club
or individual, which are largely influential in determining its or his choice, and it is in view of that
fact that I have prepared the following list of
considerations :

I. In the case of a Club which numbers among
its members many expert players, it is well to have
turf courts, as nine out of ten experts prefer them.
It may be said that a Club cannot cater to a small
class, but it must be remembered that the presence
of the most skilled players does much for the membership and general prosperity of a Club.

II. A turf court is undoubtedly more expensive,
everything considered, than one of dirt or clay. A
poor turf court is about as bad as none at all, and
one, to be kept in good condition, requires constant

supervision and care. The original cost of construction is perhaps less for a first-class turf court than one of dirt or clay, but after construction the latter requires much less attention. A consideration against the clay court, however, lies in the fact that a mixture of dirt and clay is very apt to seam or crack in the early spring, when the frost is leaving the ground. It is a matter of considerable expense to remedy such an evil, which will ordinarily be averted by carefully covering the court with boards and straw during the winter months.

III. A court of dirt or clay may be used much earlier in the spring and much sooner after a heavy rain than one of turf.

IV. In places where the soil is apt to be moist or damp, and particularly within a short distance of the sea-shore, a dirt or clay court is preferable, for if turf is used, the balls become wet and soggy and unfit for play.

V. A turf court is much cleaner and more comfortable to play upon than one of dirt, and the game, when played upon turf, is undoubtedly more picturesque and attractive for the spectator.

VI. As a rule, balls which are used on a turf court suffer less wear and tear, and therefore last longer than those which are used on dirt or clay courts.

In laying out a court it should be remembered that a large amount of space is required outside of the lines, for the ball is frequently returned so that its bound carries it some distance outside of the base or side lines. In the summer of 1889, while playing in the championship match at Newport, I made an energetic attempt to return a ball and ran at full

speed into an umpire who was seated at least twenty
feet back of the base line ; so it is probably not too
much to provide a space of at least twenty feet, or
twenty-five, if possible, back of the base line, and at
least ten feet along the side-lines.   There is nothing
more annoying to a player than to be hampered in
his movements by lack of space.   Even an old and
experienced contestant in tournaments will become
nervous when the line of spectators approaches too
close to the court.

Some care should be exercised in the selection of
a net and poles.   Cheap nets are plentiful and easy
to buy, but the purchaser will not be pleased with
his economy when he finds at the first time of using
that a ball will pass through the net almost as easily
as through the air.   It pays to purchase an expensive
net, made of the strongest material.   The top of the
net should be bounded by a band of pure white
canvas or other strong material, from three to five
inches in width, so that the player may have the best
possible view of the top of the net and direct his
strokes accordingly, for the closer to the top of the
net the ball passes, the more skillful is the stroke
considered to be.   In regard to the poles, the most
convenient style and perhaps the best in all respects
is that known as the Taylor Pole, or any other which
is constructed on similar principles.   The particular
style known as the Taylor Pole consists of a pointed
iron socket, which is driven into the ground so that
the mouth of the socket is flush with the surface, and
a pole, which is made to fit rather loosely in the
socket, and is therefore easily turned in either direction by two handles placed near the top.   As the
pole is turned to the right or left, the net rope or

wire is wound or unwound around the pole, and the net is thus easily tightened or loosened. The arrangement is simple, and the only objections which can be urged against it are : first, that the socket makes a rather large hole in the ground, and second, that the handles on the pole may intercept the ball in play, something which has occurred but once in my own experience.

The Racket and Ball are of course important equipments of the game. The Laws of Lawn Tennis require that the ball shall measure not less than $2\frac{9}{16}$ inches and not more than $2\frac{1}{2}$ inches in diameter, and that they shall weigh not less than $1\frac{15}{16}$ ounces, and not more than two ounces. An experienced player will detect any material deviation, either in measurement or weight, from the figures as laid down in the Laws. The United States National Lawn Tennis Association annually adopts, as the official ball, that one which the majority of its members considers the best in the market, and the public has a very fair guide in the opinion of so many expert players.

As for the racket, it is not at all a difficult task to select a good one, for all now manufactured are of about the same shape, and one excels another only in the quality of gut used in stringing or of the wood from which the frame is constructed. It would seem as if common sense should have dictated the adoption of the present style from the beginning of the game, but, on the contrary, the head of the racket suffered many curious and foolish changes before it took the form of the present popular shape.

The accompanying cut, No. 1, shows the old-fashioned racket with its curved head. I remember using one of them as late as 1882. It was followed in this country by many new and curious shapes, until finally the famous English racket, made by Tate, was much used by our best players, and the American manufacturers saw the necessity of introducing something similar to it. The result is shown in cut No. 2, which is the racket now in universal use, and there is no reason to believe that there will be any further change of consequence, as the present shape is the correct one from a common sense as well as scientific point of view. In regard to

No. 1.

weight, a man of ordinary strength should use a racket weighing from 13½ to 14½ ounces. In no case should one heavier than 15 ounces be used, for the lighter weights are sufficient to drive the ball with power and force, and any extra weight is only a handicap and a disadvantage.

"The Beekman," "The Sears," "The Slocum," and "The Association," are all good rackets of American make, well constructed, finely strung, and of the approved shape. I have no doubt that other good rackets are made in this country, but those which I have mentioned are most commonly used by expert players. All of them are imitations of the English "Tate," it is true, but they are so nearly, if not quite, equal

No. 2.

to the English article, that a purchaser will not suffer by encouraging the home industry.

FIG. 3. REVERSE OVERHAND SERVICE.

CHAPTER II.

THE SERVICE.

"What services canst thou do?"
                    —*King Lear.*

"The service is not service, so being done."
                    —*Cymbeline.*

I HAVE selected the Service for the contents of this chapter, inasmuch as the server begins hostilities in every game, and the subject naturally occurs to the mind as the first to be discussed. It is not proposed, however, to here treat of the advisability of a swift or slow service, the proper method of receiving, and other kindred points. All these are reserved for later discussion, and the purpose of the present chapter is simply to show the various methods of serving, the proper disposition of the different parts of the body while in the act of serving, and the relative positions of the racket and ball. The bare statement of an individual opinion does not entirely fulfill such a purpose, and I shall therefore illustrate my meaning by the use of the accompanying cuts, all of which are taken from instantaneous photographs of expert players—players who are generally considered to make the different services and strokes according to the best methods.

At the same time, it must be understood that it is extremely difficult to secure instantaneous photographs which represent the services and strokes with exactness. As the racket moves through the air, it reaches a certain position, which, if photographed, presents a very fair idea of any particular service or stroke. If the photographer is alert and catches that position, well and good ; but if there be a delay of even a small fraction of a second, the racket sweeps on in its course a n d the picture is without value to show the various characteristics of the desired stroke. The difficulty is particularly great in the case of a swift overhand service or a smash. in which the racket passes through the air at a tremendous rate of speed.

FIG. I. OVERHAND SERVICE.

In the overhand service, for instance, the racket and ball meet over the head of the server, but a photograph, which is taken the smallest fraction of a second after the meeting, shows the head of the racket within one or two feet of the ground, and conveys absolutely no idea of an overhand service.

But while some of the cuts are not entirely satisfactory, for the reasons stated, others are very nearly perfect. It is seldom that the ball can be caught, but in some of the illustrations of the service, it will be seen that the ball is clearly and sharply defined. In other cases I shall endeavor to supply the deficiency.

Perhaps I should add, in deference to the feelings of the players who were the subjects of these photographs, that little or no effort has been made to preserve a likeness to the originals, so far as the face is concerned.

It may be well, at the beginning, to explain the meaning of a few technical words which are used in connection with the service. The player who delivers the service is of course called the " server," but the one who receives it is technically known as the "striker-out." The term "fault" means that a service is not good, for some reason specified in No. 8 of the Laws of Lawn Tennis. (See Appendix.)

Law No. 6 is the only one which has any direct bearing upon the subject discussed in this chapter, and I therefore quote it, as follows :

6. **The Server** shall serve with one foot on the base line or perpendicularly above said line, and with the other foot behind said line, but not necessarily upon the ground. He shall deliver the service from the right to the left courts, alternately, beginning from the right.

The latter portion of the law, commencing with the words " he shall deliver," is not pertinent, but the remainder is important, inasmuch as it contains the only injunction found anywhere in the rules concerning the position which a player must assume in serving. The words " perpendicularly above said line " were only in recent years added to the rule, which formerly, like the English law on the subject, required the server to serve with one foot directly on the line. It naturally followed that a conscientious umpire was obliged to call a foot fault, or, in other words, call the service a bad one, if the player happened to serve with the toe of his shoe in front of the line and the heel slightly lifted from the ground, a circumstance which frequently occurred. In such a position the server practically met the requirements of the rule, but suffered through a technicality, and it was to remedy this injustice, and at the same time make the duties of the umpire less arduous and disagreeable, that the words " perpendicularly above said line " were added. The rule of course applies to all methods of serving, the only distinction being, that in some of the methods, as shown hereafter, the left foot is placed upon or above the line and the right foot behind it, while in others the positions of the feet are reversed.

The following list comprises all of the important methods of serving :

    I. Overhand Service. (Fore-handed.)

    II. Reverse Overhand Service.

    III. Underhand Twist Service. (Fore-handed.)

    IV. Underhand Twist Service. (Back-handed.)

    V. Underhand Service with Cut.

The last named would hardly be worth mentioning as a separate and distinct method were it not for the fact that this is the service which was generally used in the early days of the game, and which has since been commonly adopted by ladies. During the past few years, however, a majority of women, who have taken up the game in earnest, have cultivated an overhand service, evidently believing that the increased effectiveness of their play would more than compensate for the accompanying sacrifice of grace.

Taking up the various services in the order named, let us consider

I. *The Overhand Service.* This is the service which is most commonly used. Speed is its

FIG. 2. OVERHAND SERVICE.

chief merit. Assuming that the server is right-handed, the left foot should be placed upon the base line, and the right foot a short distance behind

it. As one stands in this position the side of
the body should be toward the net. The ball,
which is of course held in the left hand, should
be thrown straight into the air from a point about
opposite to the left arm or shoulder of the server.
The ball should be thrown at a certain distance from
the body, and that distance is about represented by
the length of the forearm and hand. At the same
time that the ball is thrown, the racket is lifted in the
air and then allowed to drop downward until the
head of the racket is about opposite to the middle of
the back. But the main point of this service is speed,
and in order to secure the greatest speed, the weight
and power of the whole body must be employed. It
follows then, that simultaneously with the throwing
of the ball and the dropping of the racket behind
the back, the weight of the body should be thrown
back upon the right foot. The head of the racket
should now be made to describe an arc, commencing
from the point behind the back, and swinging upward until it meets the ball at the highest point to
which the arm can be extended. At the same time
that the upward swing of the racket begins, the body
should once more be thrown forward, so that its
whole weight and power are exerted when the racket
and ball meet.

The height, to which the ball should be thrown,
is of course dependent upon the length of arm of the
server. The object of the overhand service is to
drive the ball downward into the service court, and
to do this it is necessary that the racket should strike
on top of the ball. It follows then, that the ball
should be thrown, so that the highest point which it
reaches will be a trifle below the highest point of

the arc described by the head of the racket. If the ball is thrown too high or too low, a swift service will almost invariably result in a fault.

Fig. 1 very fairly represents an overhand service, in which the swing from the middle of the back has begun. The ball which appears plainly, has about reached its maximum height, for although the racket seems to be a considerable distance away, it must be remembered that it is swinging through the air at lightning speed. It is probable that the server in Fig. 1 is not attempting to deliver a very swift service, for the feet are so close together, that the whole weight of the body could not properly be thrown from one to the other, as before described. When the effort is to be violent, the right foot should be about two feet behind the line.

The characteristics of a swift service are shown very plainly in Fig. 2. Here the racket and ball are almost on the point of meeting, though the latter does not appear. There is no doubt about the speed of this service. In Fig. 1, where the service is of medium pace, it is probable that the right foot will continue to rest upon the ground, when the racket strikes the ball. In Fig. 2, however, the weight of the body has been thrown forward so violently, as the racket approaches the ball, that the left foot is lifted entirely from the ground. As the ball is struck and the racket descends, the body will almost surely fall, unless the left foot is carrried forward to save it. Fig. 2 represents Mr. H. A. Taylor, who is undoubtedly one of the swiftest servers in this country. Being left-handed, he serves with the right foot upon the line and the left behind it.

II. *The Reverse Overhand Service.* This method

fails to produce the speed which is the characteristic of the ordinary overhand service, but in its place
an awkward twist is imparted to the ball. In the
ordinary method, as described, the ball takes a
straight bound after striking the ground, provided
it has been struck squarely with the face of the
racket. If not struck squarely, which is usually
the case, a twist is imparted, which causes the ball
to bound to the right of the "striker-out." The
object of the Reverse Overhand Service is to impart
a twist which shall cause the ball to bound in the
opposite direction, or to the left of the striker-out.
If this could be done with great speed, the service
would be most effective, but the twist is the most
important feature, and, as a general rule, any great
amount of twist can be secured only at a correspond-
ing sacrifice of speed. Fig. 3, at the beginning of
this chapter, admirably represents this service, as
delivered by Mr. R. D. Sears. Either of the feet may
be placed upon the line, and it is difficult to advise
one or the other, but in Fig 3, it will be seen that
Mr. Sears prefers to use the left.

The ball must be thrown in quite a different manner from that before described. First : It must be
thrown slightly farther toward the net. Second : It
must not be thrown so high, for the ball is not
struck while the arm is fully extended upward. In
Fig. 3 the ball has just left the racket, and yet the
arm is extended straight from the shoulder, with
only a slight upward tendency.

The actual swing of the racket to meet the ball,
instead of starting from the middle of the back, as in
the ordinary method, begins from a point behind
the right shoulder. From there the racket passes

in front of and rather close to the face. As it meets
the ball, which has been thrown slightly forward,
the racket is turned at an angle outward from the
body, exactly as shown in Fig. 3.

In this, as well as in every overhand service, the
racket should be grasped at the end of the handle.

III. *The Underhand Twist Service (fore-handed).*
For a slow service, this is undoubtedly the most

FIG. 4. UNDERHAND TWIST SERVICE. FORE-HANDED.)

effective which can be used. It is an exceedingly
difficult service, not only to deliver properly, but
also to clearly describe. It is chiefly used when the
server wishes to follow his service by immediately
running to the net, which occurs more often in the
double than in the single game. Dr. Dwight and
Mr. R. D. Sears are more expert in serving by this

method than any players whom I have seen, and each employs a different system.

Dr. Dwight places his left foot upon the service line and almost faces the net, but draws his racket across the ball on the *right side* of his body. Mr. Sears places either foot (usually the left) upon the line, but the other only just behind it. He faces directly toward the net and bends both knees, as shown in Fig. 4. Instead of grasping the racket at the end of the handle, as in the overhand service, he places his hand at least three or four inches from the end. The racket commences its swing from the right side of the body, the head of the racket being then about level with the waist, and passes directly *in front* of the body over to the left side. The ball is of course held in the left hand, at arm's length and exactly in front of the body. As soon as the swing of the racket begins, the ball is quietly dropped, not thrown, from the hand, and meets the racket at a point about level with the player's knees. The point of meeting would be lower were it not for the fact that the racket is grasped several inches from the end of the handle, as before described.

The racket is neither vertical nor horizontal, as it swings in front of the body. It is exactly between the two. Inasmuch as the swing begins from the side of the body, the racket naturally has a slight motion forward, which is sufficient to send the ball slowly over the net, while the lateral motion from the right side to the left imparts to the ball a tremendous amount of twist, which causes it, on striking the ground, to break sharply to the left of the striker-out.

Fig. 4 does not represent Mr. Sears in the act of

delivering this service, but it shows his method with considerable accuracy. The right foot should perhaps be a little nearer the line, and the hand should be grasping the racket at a greater distance from the end of the handle. With these slight exceptions, this cut presents a very fair picture of the beginning of an underhand twist service. The racket has just begun to swing from the side, and the ball, which plainly appears, has already been dropped from the hand.

IV. *Underhand Twist Service (backhanded).* This is exactly the reverse of the service just described, both in method and result. Here the right foot is usually placed upon the line, and the racket commences its swing from the left side of the body. It passes in front of

FIG. 5. UNDERHAND SERVICE WITH CUT.

the body and over to the right side, meeting the ball exactly as before. The lateral motion from the left side to the right imparts a twist, which causes the ball to break to the right of the striker-out.

V. *Underhand Service with Cut.* This method of serving is comparatively unimportant, and yet at times may be extremely effective. In playing upon

soft or wet turf, for instance, I should prefer to be
served a swift overhand service rather than an underhand cut.

Fig. 5 shows the position of the server just prior
to the delivery of this service. The left foot is
placed upon the line and the side of the body is
toward the net, as in the overhand service. The ball
is merely dropped from the hand, as the racket is
brought forward to meet it. The racket is held in
such a manner (see Fig. 5), that instead of striking
squarely against the side of the ball, it goes slightly
underneath it. The motion of the ball is not thus
affected so that it bounds to one side or the other, as
in the underhand twist services. The bound is
straight, but the ball rises only a very short distance
from the ground, and in this lies the only value of
the underhand cut. It can readily be seen that it is
most effective upon a court of soft turf, where the
very nature of the ground assists it.

Fig. A. FOREHAND STROKE (OFF THE GROUND).

CHAPTER III.

THE STROKE.

"Methinks, I play, as I have seen them do."
—*A Winter's Tale.*

LAWN TENNIS strokes, in general, may be either *ground strokes* or *volleys*. A *volley* is any return of the ball before it reaches the ground, while a *ground stroke* is any return from the bound of the ball. A *half-volley* is really a ground stroke, for the ball is not returned until after it has struck the ground; but it is the theory of the stroke that the racket should meet the ball at almost the same moment as the ball strikes the ground, and it is therefore not inaptly termed a half-volley.

All strokes, whether volleys or ground strokes, may be either *forehand* or *backhand*. A forehand stroke (for a right-handed man) is one in which the arm swings on the right side of the body. A backhand stroke is any stroke in which the racket meets the ball on the left side, the arm swinging across or in front of the body.

Again, all strokes, whether volleys or ground strokes, may be made with or without *cut*. A stroke without cut is made by meeting the ball squarely with the head of the racket, or, in other words, by holding the racket so that the head forms an exact right angle to the course of the ball. If a cut is desired, the racket must be held so that the head forms an angle, greater than a great angle, to the course of the ball. When the ball meets the racket held in this position, it is given such a motion that it rises only a short distance from the ground at the end of the return, and in this lies the chief value of the cut.

The following list comprises all of the important strokes:

    I. The forehand stroke (off the ground).
    II. The backhand stroke (off the ground).
    III. The forehand volley.
    IV. The backhand volley.
    V. The forehand half-volley.
    VI. The backhand half-volley.
    VII. The smash.

Before going into a separate analysis of each, let us first consider certain characteristics which are common to all of these strokes when they are executed in good form. The word *form*, as used in this connection, is a general term, which may be concisely defined as the method of play. When we speak of a man as playing in good form or bad form, we mean that he does or does not play according to the best methods, or, rather, those methods which the success and experience of expert players have demonstrated to be the best. The disposition of the feet, the swing of the arm, the use of the eye, the general carriage of the body—all these are considered under the general term form.

Mr. R. D. Sears, champion of the United States for seven successive years, is said to have advised the Lawn Tennis player "to keep his eyes on the ball, and his feet on the ground." Whether it was our popular ex-champion or some other who delivered himself of this sage advice, it is certain that two excellent principles of good form are therein laid down. The use of Mr. Sears' name in this connection is an unpleasant reminder of his enforced retirement from Lawn Tennis competition. His participation was of practical value to the game, for inexperienced players, by merely watching his play, were often able to secure a complete lesson in good form.

Taking up these characteristics

Fig. B. END OF DROP STROKE.

which are common to all strokes, it may first be laid down as a general rule that no stroke should be made with the two feet together. In every case it is customary and necessary to take a step forward with either one foot or the other, and the length of the step is almost always proportionate to the amount of body power which must be infused into the stroke. The latter principle is illustrated by the fact that in making a backhand stroke, in which the wrist and forearm play the most important part, the feet are a much shorter distance apart than they are in the forehand drive, which, to be effective, must be made with speed, and to

Fig. C. BACK-HAND STROKE (OFF THE GROUND).

secure speed the power of the body must be used to back up the strength of the arm.

The reason for the rule is obvious. As the arm swings forward in a stroke, the body naturally accompanies it. The natural balance of the body will be destroyed unless one of the feet is thrust forward to save it. If the exertion is violent, the foot must be extended further, as in the forehand

drive. If the body is but little used, as in the backhand stroke, only a short step is necessary.

Again, it is a universal rule that the step must be
taken with the foot which is most far removed
from the racket. Thus, in any forehand stroke, the
step is taken with the left foot, while in any backhand stroke it is the right foot which is used.

Fig. D. END OF LOW FOREHAND VOLLEY.

These illustrations of course apply only when the
player is right-handed, for if he happens to be left-
handed the positions of the feet are reversed, as
will be observed in some of the accompanying cuts,
which represent a left-handed player. Right-
handed or left-handed, however, the general rule is
of course the same—the step is taken with the foot

most far removed from the racket at the beginning
of the stroke.

As the stroke is completed, the foot which is
behind is now brought forward to join the other,
and the body is once more upon a firm footing and
prepared for another movement in any direction.
The player will be best prepared for the next
movement if the body is thrown somewhat forward
and the knees slightly bent. In such a position
the next step, in whatever direction it may be, can
be taken with the least possible friction.

Another important element of form is the management of the racket, and the arm which wields it.
The racket should be grasped at the end of the
handle, unless an extraordinary amount of cut is
desired, and then the hand may properly be placed
at some distance from the end; but such a stroke
belongs to Tennis rather than Lawn Tennis. The
hand should grasp the handle firmly, but not
tightly, for its position in a forehand stroke differs
from that which it assumes in a backhand stroke,
and the change must necessarily be sudden and
rapid. It is true that a few good players claim
that the position of the hand should not, and in
their own cases does not, change, but it is difficult
to understand how both strokes can be thus made
in good form. For a forehand stroke, I suppose
that about every player grasps the racket in the
same manner. The fingers and thumb meet in
front, and the body of the hand is behind the
handle, where it can best give power to the stroke.
For a backhand stroke, however, various changes
are made by different players. My own method is
to allow the body of the hand to slip from the back

to the side of the handle, and to place the thumb along the back, in which position I find it a most useful aid in giving direction to the return.

The swing of the racket before meeting the ball should not be long or particularly violent; for, if the strength of the arm and body is properly used, the length of the swing adds but little to the power of the return, and may do much to injure the accuracy or squareness with which the ball is struck. The arm itself should swing easily and freely, each joint being given full play. Making a stroke with a stiff or cramped arm is a most common fault.

Let us now take up the different strokes in their order, as before given, and consider each separately:

I. *The Forehand Stroke* (off the ground). To make this stroke perfectly, the player should be at such a distance back from the point where the ball strikes the ground that his racket will meet the ball on its descent from the bound. The stroke

Fig. E. FOREHAND VOLLEY.

should be made, that is, the racket and ball should meet, when the ball has nearly reached the ground for a second time, the arm then being stretched to its full length and moving freely in a plane parallel and close to the side of the body. The advantage of a stroke made in this manner over one in which the arm is allowed to swing out from the body

Fig. F. BACKHAND VOLLEY.

(commonly called a round-arm stroke) is obvious. When the arm swings straight and close to the body, the hand and the eye are brought into a close union, and the ball is directed with much certainty; but if the arm is rounded, and the hand thereby removed from the plane parallel to the side of the body, the aim and direction of the return are seriously affected, just as they would be in the case of a marksman who, in using a rifle, should hold it at a distance from the body instead of sighting with his eye along the barrel.

The step forward is taken with the left foot and is usually quite long, for the body-power is largely

Fig. G. FOREHAND HALF-VOLLEY.

exerted in making this stroke. Fig A, at the beginning of this chapter, shows the racket at about the exact position in which it meets the ball. The figure represents the stroke just as I have described it, except that the arm, instead of being fully extended downward, appears to be somewhat bent at the elbow. This apparent inaccuracy will shortly be explained.

In the ordinary forehand stroke the head of the racket is brought squarely against the ball. More or less cut, however, has always been used by good players in making the stroke, and during recent years another element has been added which has made practically a new stroke. The new stroke is that which is commonly known as the *drop stroke*. The general movement of the body and racket are the same as in the ordinary forehand stroke, until the racket and ball meet. At this moment, however, the racket is drawn vertically upward. The swing of the racket forward sends the ball over the net, while the vertical movement upward gives it a rotary motion through the air, which causes it to shoot suddenly and sharply downward as soon as it has passed the net. The scientific principle involved will be recognized as the same as that which the Base-ball pitcher employs in throwing a drop curve, or, as the Base-ballists sometimes call it, a " down-shoot."

The player in Fig. A is lifting his racket upward, but unless the movement is made with more violence than it appears to be in this photograph, but little drop can be secured. The extent of the drop is proportionate to the violence and suddenness with which the racket is lifted. Indeed, the fact that this stroke, in its most effective form, can not be made easily and quietly, constitutes perhaps the only objection to its use. The extra exertion which must necessarily be employed leaves the player in an unfortunate position at the end of the stroke, a fact which is plainly demonstrated in Fig. B. It is only fair to add, however, that this figure does not accurately represent the end of a drop stroke, as it is usually made. The player, whom the figure represents, is very successful with the stroke, but executes it in a manner somewhat different from that described. At the same time that he lifts his racket upward, he also turns it at an angle inward toward the body; or, in other words, at an angle the reverse of that at which he would hold it, if he desired to cut. It is difficult to see how this extra movement can add to the effectiveness of the stroke, and it is that feature, more than any other, which finally brings the racket into the curious position shown in Fig. B.

II. *The Backhand Stroke* (off the ground). The step forward is here taken with the right foot. The step need not be long, for but little body-power is used.

Fig. II. BACKHAND HALF-VOLLEY.

The shifting of the racket to the left side of the body is simultaneous with the beginning of the step. At the end of this movement the hand and forearm lie close to the front of the body, and form a right angle to the upper arm. The swing to meet the ball is made almost entirely with the forearm. The racket and ball should meet at the moment when the arm is once more completely straight. The actual point of meeting should be well in front of the body, and about on a line with the left leg.

When the meeting occurs at that point, the hand which holds the racket is directly in front of the body, and a close union of the hand and eye is again secured.

Fig. C is not a satisfactory representation of the stroke, for several reasons. In the first place the bound of the ball was so short that the player, in order to reach it, was obliged to take an unusually long step. Again, the ball has already been struck, and the picture shows the position of the racket at the very end of the stroke.

III. and IV. *The Forehand and Backhand Volleys.* In making a low forehand volley—that is, one where the racket and ball meet at any point below the players's knee—the same methods should be employed as those already described in connection with the forehand stroke off the ground. The arm should swing in a plane parallel to the side of the body, and, if a drop is desired, the racket must be lifted in the same manner as described (page 40). A cut also adds much to the effectiveness of a low forehand volley. The step is of course taken with the left foot, and the swing of the racket to meet the ball should be even shorter and less violent than in making a forehand stroke off the ground. In making any volley the racket should be brought forward quietly, for the mere impact of the ball against the tightly strung racket is sufficient to send it back with considerable speed.

Fig. D shows the racket at the end of a low forehand volley. A low backhand volley is made in about the same way as a backhand stroke off the ground (page 41).

In actual play, however, low volleys are not often made. The back-court player has practically no volleying to do, while the tendency of those who favor a volleying game is to approach so close to the net that they are able to meet the ball while it is at least three feet (the height of the net) from the ground. The great majority of volleys are therefore between the waist and shoulder, and here the methods which have been described can no longer be employed. In making a forehand volley between the waist and shoulder, the racket and ball must meet at a considerable distance from the body. But the point of meeting should not be directly at the side of the body, for in that case the hand is drawn completely out of union with the eye. This union can still be somewhat preserved if the stroke is made at a considerable distance in front of the body, exactly as shown in Fig. E. That figure is my idea of a forehand volley, when executed in perfect form. It will be observed that the racket is meeting the ball with little or no cut, and that the wrist is playing a most important part in the stroke. The player is Mr. R. L. Beeckman.

In the backhand volley the union of hand and eye is again perfectly secured, for if the stroke is made, as shown in Fig. F, the hand remains almost on a line with the eye, and may direct the ball with an unerring aim. Here again it is seen that the stroke is made almost entirely with the forearm and wrist.

V. *The Forehand Half-Volley.* This stroke is to be

used only when the return can be made in no other
way. This necessity usually arises when the ball
strikes directly at your feet. If you can volley by
stepping forward a step or two, it is, as a general
rule, better to do this than to resort to the half-
volley. On the other hand, it is generally better to
make the half-volley
rather than step
backward in order
to receive the ball
on the bound. In
making the latter
movement the
weight of the body
must be thrown *back-
ward*, and this vio-
lates a general rule
of good form, which
requires that in mak-
ing any stroke the
weight of the body
should be thrown
forward.

There is room for
some difference of
opinion as to how a
half - volley should
be made. The idea

Fig. K. BACKHAND SMASH.

of the stroke is that the racket should meet the ball
at the very beginning of the latter's bound from
the ground. Some players think that the racket
should be brought down on the ball with a chop,
but it is difficult to see how an accurate return can
be made in that way. The best method, in my

opinion, is as follows: the racket should be low-
ered until it almost touches the ground at a point
perhaps two feet, or thereabouts, from where the
ball will probably strike. The racket is then brought
forward along and close to the ground to meet the
ball. The motion of the arm is very much the
same as in the ordinary forehand stroke off the
ground. It is fully extended downward and swings
close to the body. Fig. G quite accurately represents this idea of the stroke. In that representation the racket will meet the ball at a point about
on a line with the left foot. It will be noticed that
the step is unusually long. This is because the
stroke is made well in front of the body, and at the
same time close to the ground. The body inclines
forward more than in any other stroke, and the
step must be unusually long in order to preserve
the balance.

VI. *The Backhand Half-Volley.* Fig. H represents
this stroke when made in the same way as the forehand half-volley just described. The racket and
ball meet almost in front of the body, and the hand
which wields the racket is directly in line with the
eye. The player shown in Fig. H is left-handed, and
the step is therefore taken with the left foot.

VII. *The Smash.* When we speak of *smashing a
ball* it means, to those who are untutored in Lawn
Tennis methods, nothing more than striking the
ball with an unusual amount of violence and force.
But the technical meaning of the smash, as a stroke,
is quite different. It is a term which is usually
applied to any hard volley from above the shoulder.
If a ball strikes the ground and bounds above your
head, there is no reason why your return of that

ball, provided it is made with force and directed downward into the opposite court, should not be called a smash. But smashes, as a general rule, are volleys in which the racket meets the ball at nearly the highest point to which the arm can extend it. A smash is nothing more than an overhand service (Fig. 2, Chap. II.), except that the service is delivered at the base line, while the smash is generally made at or near the net. The purpose of both the service and the smash is to direct the ball swiftly downward into the opposite court, but as the smash is usually made from a point near the net, it follows that the racket should strike more on top of the ball than it does in the service. This is about the only point of difference between the two.

A smash may be made either forehanded or backhanded. A backhand smash is but little used, for an agile player will usually find time to place himself upon the left of the ball and smash forehanded. The whole strength of the body may be thrown into a forehand smash, while the arm alone almost entirely performs the work of the other. (Fig. K.)

Richard D. Sears

CHAPTER IV.

THE SINGLE GAME.

"Let them play.—Play, sirs."
—*King Henry IV.*

ASSUMING that the reader is acquainted with the rules, and that he is now familiar with the different services and strokes, I shall attempt to give a few practical ideas, in this and the following chapters, about the actual playing of the game. Although the present chapter is supposed to treat of the single game, it will, without doubt, contain some ideas equally applicable to the double game, which will be separately considered in a later chapter. It may be proper to add, that I shall endeavor. in this chapter, to set forth these points in rather a general way only. The reader will perhaps find some of the same ideas, but together with others, in greater detail and possibly in more practical form, in the succeeding chapter, which is addressed particularly to young beginners.

Taking up these ideas in their natural order. we first consider

THE SERVICE.

And here the point most commonly discussed is whether or not speed is essential or desirable. I have always been mildly opposed to the use of a very swift service in the single game, on the ground that it was an almost useless expenditure of energy. My own service is decidedly weak, but I hardly think that I have allowed that fact to influence my opinion upon the question, as one of policy. It is true that a swift service will score many aces against an inferior player, but it is equally true that a player of only average ability cares nothing for the speed with which you may serve, provided the ball falls within his reach. A swift service requires a violent effort, which must have some effect upon the endurance. A service of moderate speed economizes strength, and at the same time may be placed out of the reach of the striker-out, if well directed. Again, the player who serves with moderate speed will make his first service good four times out of five, while the swift server will serve faults in the same proportion and be compelled to fall back upon a slow second service. And, finally, the swift server is much more likely to make double faults.

Dr. Dwight, however, favors speed, mainly because the striker-out is afraid or unable to *place* his return of a swift service, and the advantage thus gained by the server will probably win him the point in the next two or three strokes. There are some few players, too, who appear to have a peculiar ability to serve with great swiftness and still make few faults. Such an ability seems to be more or less of a knack. To possess it one need not have great strength of arm, for strong-armed men are often weak servers. While a tall man naturally has an advantage, height is not a necessity. Mr. H. A. Taylor, who is much below the average in stature, is in my opinion one of the swiftest and most successful servers in the country. The ball seems to leave his racket as if shot out of a cannon, and yet there is nothing peculiar about his method except that he starts from a point behind the base line and takes two or three steps before swinging his racket, instead of standing with one foot upon the line, which is usually done. The danger of such a method is in the liability to make foot faults.

When playing a match, if I win the toss and there is but little choice between courts, I usually compel my adversary to serve, not on account of my own weak service, but because I am anxious to play at the net; and I can usually secure such a position upon my return of the service. If my adversary happens to have a very severe service, such as Taylor's, I may perhaps be unable to return it so that I can run to the net, but I still compel him to serve, in the hope that his first services may be faults. If you wish to pursue the policy of running to the net on your own service (a policy which is almost universally condemned by good players), you should serve a very slow service, with a cut or twist, if possible, so that you may be well up toward the net when your adversary makes his return. These last few ideas about service bring us naturally to the consideration of a question which has been much discussed. As a general rule, which is the more profitable policy to adopt,—

The Net Game, or The Back-Court Game?

The substance of this inquiry is about as follows : is it sound policy to run to the net at every possible opportunity, or is it, as a general rule, preferable to remain in the back of the court ? If you adopt the first policy, you rely upon accurate volleying and an occasional smash to win the point ; if the second, you may score by passing your adversary (assuming that he is playing at the net), or by skillful and well-timed "lobbing." It naturally occurs to a well-balanced mind, that a judicious mixture of the two policies, each being used as occasion requires, would be most proper. This is undoubtedly true, but the trouble is that different players have different opinions about the requirements of a particular occasion. One may think it proper to run to the net, when another may prefer to remain at the base line, and thus these two methods of playing have grown to be separate and distinct policies, each having its adherents and followers.

In the earlier days of the game, it was the custom for both players to stand at the back of the court, and return each ball from the bound. If I remember aright, it is the Renshaws who are given the credit for the idea, at least in its perfection, of returning the ball before it reaches the ground, and it was their accurate volleying and hard smashing, which brought them at once to the front in England, where they have remained the champions for many years. Their style of course found many imitators, both in their own country and ours, and I think that it has been the general idea among the best players of the United States during the past few years, that under ordinary conditions a good volleyer could

easily defeat a first-class back-court player. Some,
in fact, have been so enthusiastic, that they may
properly be called extremists upon the question.

The most notable of these is perhaps Mr. O. S.
Campbell, a young but prominent player who performed most brilliantly in a recent Championship
Tournament at Newport. Mr. Campbell's play is
chiefly remarkable for strong and accurate volleying,
and his fondness for net play is so great, that he almost invariably runs to the net on his own service,
a practice which is usually considered suicidal. We
shall probably never again have the opportunity of
seeing the two types of game opposed to each other
under such striking circumstances, as when Mr.
Campbell and Mr. E. G. Meers, a well-known English player, met in the tournament of which I have
just spoken. Mr. Campbell was about eighteen
years of age, almost a boy, while Mr. Meers never
touched a racket until he was forty. Mr. Meers had
come from England with the praiseworthy intention
of taking back our Championship Cup, if possible,
while Mr. Campbell was fired with the idea of pre-
venting such a proceeding, if he could. Campbell
played a perfect volleying game, while Meers was
the typical back-court player, rarely going to the
net unless circumstances compelled it. Under such
conditions, then, it was quite a triumph for Campbell and the style of game which he represented, that
long before the finish of the hard fought contest, he
had compelled his adversary to adopt his own tactics,
including even the running to the net on a service.
Mr. Meers would probably claim that this match
hardly afforded a fair test of the merits of the two
styles of game, inasmuch as he was playing in a

strange country and under conditions of temperature and atmosphere differing from those to which he was accustomed. This may be true, but I think that a majority of the spectators, who thoroughly understood Lawn Tennis, agreed that Mr. Meers was the more skillful of the two players, and that he was defeated only because he persisted, until too late, in playing a back-court game against the brilliant volleying of Mr. Campbell.

We were told by Mr. Meers that the present tendency of English players is toward a return to the base-line game. My own opinion is decidedly in favor of the net game. I should never run to the net on my own service; but I almost always attempt to do so on my return of an adversary's service, and am willing to take great risks otherwise in order to secure the position at the net. In regard to the exact point at which you should stand when playing at the net, I think that nearly midway between the service line and the net is the proper place. At that point you will be near enough to smash and volley with force, few balls will strike at your feet, you are least likely to be passed, and there is but little danger that the ball will be "lobbed" over your head.

USE OF MENTAL POWERS IN LAWN TENNIS.

Some years ago it was quite common to regard Lawn Tennis as a game requiring so little physical effort that it could afford amusement only for women, children and effeminate men. This idea was soon effectually dispelled, but even at the present time many, who are unfamiliar with the game, persist in thinking that it consists of nothing more than knocking a ball back and forth across a net, and that

there is no occasion for the use of the head in such a
simple proceeding. There could not be a more mis-
taken idea. Physical strength is necessary as a
foundation, but, in addition, determination, confidence, coolness, steadiness, pluck, perseverance, pa-
tience, close observation, self-control, method — all
these, among others, are mental qualities which are
thoroughly tested and trained in this game, and all
of which, in a greater or less degree, go to make up
the successful Lawn Tennis player.

All other conditions being equal between two
players, it is not too much to say that the one who
is most thoroughly determined and has the most
complete confidence will gain the victory. Circumstances rarely arise when it pays to be other than
aggressive. A defensive policy has never won many
matches at Lawn Tennis. On the other hand, it is
not right to adopt an aggressive policy in a fiery and
hot-headed way. The value of coolness, steadiness
and self-control can not be over-estimated. Lawn
Tennis is a wonderfully quick game. In the midst
of a rally, a player has no time to stop and consider
what he shall do next. Thought and action must
be almost·simultaneous. As a natural consequence,
it is more than common for a player of little experience to become excited and lose his head, or to be
"rattled," as we usually term this failing. The
"rattled" player is often unable to make a stroke.
It is perhaps true that only long experience will
completely remedy such a trouble, but there are
certain points, nevertheless, which I think should be
of some assistance to a man who is easily unnerved.
In the first place, he should play as slow a game as
possible. I do not mean that he should be inactive

in his movements during a rally or "rest";* but between the "rests" he should take time to consider that the performance in which he is engaged is not of so much importance, after all, and that there is little need of growing excited about it. Then again, he should never be *in great haste* to score a point. In the midst of a rally, he sees an opportunity to score by making an extraordinary effort; he takes his chances and attempts to be brilliant, but it is quite probable that the ball is not directed exactly as he intended, or perhaps his adversary may make a skillful return ; the ball comes back, our excitable friend becomes discouraged at the result of his great effort, and is thus well on the road toward a bad case of "rattle." How much better if he had been patient and steady ; if he had allowed the risky chance to go by and waited for the sure one, which must have come later !

There are certain annoyances, however, which must severely test the self-control of the most unexcitable player. The ball may take an erratic bound, a spectator may approach too close to the court and interfere with a stroke, or, most annoying of all, an umpire may err in his judgment at the most exciting stage of the game. Under such circumstances, it is of course difficult to restrain the angry passions, but the ability and power to do so should be carefully cultivated, for the loss of self-control only adds fuel to the flame. It should be remembered that such misfortunes may happen to one as well as another, and that if you suffer from them at one time, it will be "evened up" at the expense of your adversary later on. In regard to annoyances from umpires, it

---

* "Rest" is the equivalent of "rally."

may be said that many of these are the result of ignorance as to their duties rather than a failure of eyesight ; as for instance, it happens quite often that an umpire calls out "good ball," and the player understands him as saying "fault," which is directly the opposite. For this reason an umpire should be selected not only for his good eyesight, but also on account of his knowledge of the requirements of the position, the chief requirement being that he should not open his mouth while the ball is in play, except to say "fault," "let," "out," or "not up," meaning by the last named expression that the ball had not been returned until it had struck the ground for a second time.

The average player does not appreciate the importance of perseverance or constant effort. Whether you are away ahead or far behind, the principle is the same. Lawn Tennis is a game with many queer turns and surprises, and many a player, having secured a good lead, and loafing along in fancied security, is suddenly awakened to the fact that his adversary, by continual perseverance, has "struck a new gait" and is rapidly overhauling him. It is then too late, for experience teaches the Lawn Tennis player that the hardest time in the world to "brace" is when his opponent is gaining. I can think of no better illustration of this point than a match in Doubles, which was played at Narragansett Pier by H. A. Taylor and myself, against O. S. Campbell and R. P. Huntington, Jr. Taylor and I had won the first two sets with ease, mainly on account of the poor play of the other side, and the score of the third and what might have been the final set, was 5 to 4, and forty love in our favor. We therefore needed only one point to win, and probably could have gained it in one of the next three strokes if we had made concerted effort, or if the fear of defeat had entered our minds. Almost before we could realize it, the set was lost, and during the next two, try as we could, it seemed impossible to "brace," while our adversaries played with renewed courage. They won both sets and the match, and all because they had persevered even at the moment of almost certain defeat.

I doubt that an experienced player ever goes into an important match without having previously thought out a plan of action. The man who plays without method or aim is never a success. It will never do, however, to adopt a fixed policy and use it against all alike. A victory is as often won by an attack upon the weak points of an adversary as by using your own strong points. You should therefore closely observe the methods of those to whom you are opposed, detect their failings, and frame your own policy accordingly. If your adversary, for instance, is weak in back-hand play, and likely to become discouraged at his own failures, you should continually attack that weakness in his game. The championship match at Newport, in the summer of 1889, was won by exactly such a method. In that contest I allowed my usually skillful adversary, Mr. Shaw, to defeat himself by his own errors, and he did it very easily, too. The result might have been far different if his great weakness in back-hand play had not discouraged and annoyed him.

In Lawn Tennis, however, as in all other sports, Experience is the great teacher. Two hours of practice with an experienced and skillful player is worth more than two chapters of advice.

James Dwight.

CHAPTER V.

HINTS TO YOUNG BEGINNERS.*

> " Nay,
> You shall find no boys' play here, I can tell
> you."
>
> —*King Henry IV.*

Part I.

LAWN TENNIS is a game in which there is more opportunity for skill and science than the ordinary observer imagines. There must always be a considerable difference of opinion as to how certain plays should be made, and so it is with some hesitation that I shall attempt to give a few points to young beginners. I shall assume that you are acquainted with the rudiments of the game, and that you are about to play a set with some imaginary adversary. I shall look on and give you a few hints, founded not only upon my own experience in playing, but also upon my observation of other more skillful players.

And now let us suppose that you are commencing

---

* Reprinted by permission from "Harper's Young People."

the set. Suppose you take the service. And first, where should you stand to serve? You must be governed somewhat by the position and strength of your adversary, but it is safe to lay it down as a general rule that the most advantageous position is as near as possible to the centre of the base line. In that position you will not only the better protect your own court, but you will also worry your antagonist much more than in any other. Watch him closely, and if you think him weak backhanded, be sure to serve to his backhand. In receiving your first service, he must of course be standing in the right-hand court. If he foolishly betrays his weakness in backhand play by edging over to the left, so that he may receive your service on his forehand, then a very easy service to the right hand corner of the court will be out of his reach. Don't try to put too much speed in your service, unless you are very anxious to make one particular point. Then "let her go." But, as a general rule, a very swift service is, in my opinion, a waste of energy; it is apt to strain the muscles of the shoulder, and is really not so difficult to return as one of moderate speed, but placed in an unguarded portion of the service court, which is really a much larger space to serve into than it appears to be. Take this, then, as a general rule in serving: always attempt to *place* the service in an unguarded corner, but not with great speed, and never, by any chance, allow yourself to make a double fault.

And now, no matter how much care you devote to your service, the chances are ten to one, if you are playing with a good player, that the ball will come back to you. What, then, should be your position after serving? When you serve from the middle of the base line, as I advised, you should remain standing at about that point, but ready to spring immediately to whichever side of the court your opponent may return the ball. I know that some of the most skillful players would tell you at this point that there are occasions when it pays to run to the net, or, rather, toward it, immediately after serving. Now there is no difference of opinion as to this point, viz., that a spot somewhere between the service line and the net, where the ball may be best taken on a volley, is the proper place to stand, when you can get there from the position of serving without running a serious risk of losing the point on the way. It seems to me that you encounter even more than that serious risk in attempting, on any occasion, to run up *immediately* after serving. I never do it myself, except by way of experiment; and at the risk of running counter to the opinion of more experienced players than myself, I should advise you never to attempt it. Be patient and wait, but bear in mind all the time that that spot between the service line and the net is where you ought to be as soon as you can safely get there. If you can toss the ball high in the air and toward the back of your opponent's court, do so by all means at the first opportunity, and then run up as fast as you can, so as to be firm in your position when the ball comes back. Again, if you think that you have driven the ball so successfully from the back of the court, that your opponent must make a weak return, then, too, run up and take that return on a volley.

Up to this point I have been assuming that your opponent ran toward the net immediately after returning your service. If he does not do so (and in only one contingency, of which I shall speak hereafter, is it entirely proper that he should not), then you must at once take advantage of this fact, and follow your very first return by running swiftly toward the net, for if you wait even for one return, your adversary may have recovered himself and reached the much coveted position.

And now suppose that you have served your game out, and taken a position to receive the service of your adversary. What should that position be? As to how far back from the service line it should be, that distance must of course be proportioned to the speed of the service which you are to receive. If your adversary has a very swift service, you may be obliged to stand back of the base line, and when in that position you must watch carefully to see that he does not fool you by dropping a very slow service just over the net. But it seems to me that it is more important to consider your position with relation to the side and centre lines of the court. If you are weak backhanded, don't betray that weakness just before receiving a service by edging over toward the centre-line so as to receive the service on your forehand. If you do this, a sharp opponent will not only place the service in the extreme right hand corner, out of your reach, but also, and of far more importance, he will thus at the very outset obtain knowledge of a fatal weakness in your game, and place four out of every five balls on your backhand.

It must be your aim to return the service so that the ball will drop just as close as possible to the base line of your opponent's court. Don't try to return it too swiftly, for it takes a Renshaw to put great speed in the return, and yet cause the ball to strike within a few inches of the base line. You and I should be satisfied, at least until we have played longer, to strike near the base line, without attempting great speed. If you can place the ball close to either side line, and at the same time far back toward the base line, well and good; you are making a brilliant return. But don't become too adventurous, for in the struggle to return the ball so close to so many lines, there is just a chance you may place it outside the court.

And why is it so important to make your return fall close to the base line? First, because it embarrasses your opponent in his stroke; and second, it gives you just so much more time in which to follow your return by running toward the net. I know that almost all of our expert players agree in considering this of the utmost importance. You must start immediately after returning the service, and be firmly intrenched in your proper position between the net and service line by the time the ball comes back. You will remember that I spoke of one contingency, and only one, in which it would not be proper to run to the net after the first return. This is when you see that your return is not well directed toward the base line, but will fall, perhaps, within the service line of your opponent's court. This must happen sometimes to the best of players, and in such a case it becomes so easy for your adversary to place his return

on either side of you, if you are at the net, that
discretion is distinctly "the better part of valor,"
and you will do well to retire to the back of the
court and await another chance to run up. We
can lay down no general rule to govern this play,
but it is of such vital importance to reach the position at the net that I should advise you to run up
even if your first return falls only eight or ten feet
back of the service line. I may be wrong; you
certainly run great risk of being "passed," as it is
called, but in this case I believe that the importance of the position sought for justifies the risk.

Perhaps your opponent may be one of those who
believe in sometimes running toward the net immediately after serving. If he tries it with you,
don't become excited when you see him running
up; keep cool, and you have him at your mercy.
There are two plays you may make, either of which
will bother him exceedingly. First, return the
service down the side line. Do not seek for much
speed in this return, for you must remember that
your adversary is coming forward swiftly, and it is
impossible for him to turn either to the right or
left for more than a very short distance. If he is
swiftly approaching the net through the middle of
the court, a ball of moderate speed down the side
line will be out of his reach. But watch him
closely, and if he anticipates your stroke down the
side, and so approaches the net along that side,
then he must leave the remaining portion of the
court unguarded, and as he runs up you can easily
place the ball across the court in front of him,
unless you lose your head at the approach of the
enemy, and allow yourself to become "rattled."

I think that we have now covered nearly all of the points which arise when you are serving or receiving a service, and the rest of the set is mainly a repetition of these points. Let us now consider the method of play generally, and if possible pick up one or two hints. And first, it seems to me that the the importance of lobbing, or tossing, as it is more commonly called, is not sufficiently impressed upon the minds of beginners. They are apt to regard the tossing of the ball high in the air as "baby play," where is, in reality, it is one of the most important and effective strokes of the game. There are two kinds of lobs, and each, of course, is to be played only when your adversary is at the net. First, a low toss, which will go just over your opponent's head, and which you do not intend him to return; and second, a high one, which you may use when you wish to worry him, and test his endurance by making him run to the back of the court to return the ball. The amount of exertion required to run to the back of the court, return the ball, and then go back to the net again at the first opportunity, must sooner or later exhaust the strongest of men, so that the importance of the lob, or toss, can be readily appreciated.

A question often considered is the amount of practice which a player should have in order to show a steady improvement in his game. There is no doubt that practice up to a certain point is almost as important to a Lawn Tennis player as to a lawyer. But beyond that certain point it will not only not help to improve, but sometimes even cause him to fall off in his game. You have all heard of a player "growing stale," which means simply that

he has had too much playing. No general rule can
be laid down, but you can at least keep your eyes
open, and when you see that you have ceased to
improve your game, stop playing for a time; give
yourself a good rest, and then begin again. Above
all, don't practice aimlessly, or merely with the
idea of beating your opponent. Think of some
points of play in which you wish particularly to
improve, and practice those points. In other
words, play with some method, and try hard to
make the head a valuable assistant to the arm.

And here it may not be improper to make one
suggestion. In Lawn Tennis, more than in any
other game, without doubt, is there opportunity for
the courteous and considerate treatment of an adversary. Always bear this in mind; and then even
if you lose the game, you will have the consolation
of knowing that you are winning respect and popularity.

PART II.

IN order to show a steady improvement in any
game, one must seek to overcome his most
prominent faults and weaknesses. In Lawn Tennis
particularly, there are many faults which are common to all beginners. I shall now attempt to point
out some of those faults, and if possible suggest
proper remedies.

And first let us consider what is ordinarily called
"form." You have often heard a Lawn Tennis
player spoken of as playing in "good form" or
"bad form." I remember reading in *Harper's
Young People*, about two years ago, an article on
Lawn Tennis, in which the writer stated that "the

first thing to be cultivated or acquired by a young beginner is grace." We all agree upon this point, but I am afraid that you may misunderstand the meaning of the word "grace," used in this sense. I take it that the writer did not mean that you should cultivate "grace" in your movements in order that you might win the admiration and applause of spectators. If you cultivate grace for such a purpose, then you are cultivating a serious fault, for your game will surely lose in strength. But I know that the writer, in using the term "grace," meant something which I prefer to call "good form." As a Lawn Tennis player, you must cultivate "good form," which means, among other things, that you must endeavor to give a free and easy movement to the arm which holds the racket. Almost all beginners, and some who have played for years, are apt to use their arms just as if they had no elbow joints and no wrist joints. This is particularly noticeable in making a backhand stroke. It is more than common to see players make this stroke with the arm perfectly straight and stiff; whereas, to make it correctly, both the elbow joint and the wrist joint should be given full play, and almost all of the work should be done by the wrist and forearm. The arm should be used somewhat as the elocution-master at school tries to teach you to use it in making gestures. Perhaps the best specimen of this "free-arm play," as it is called, is seen in the game of Thomas Pettitt, the professional Court Tennis player. If you could see him play, you would understand the method much better than I can now explain it.

It is certainly a fact that every player, attempting

Lawn Tennis for the first time, finds that he is wofully weak in the backhand stroke. The forehand is a natural stroke; the backhand is an acquired one. This can hardly be called a fault; it is a weakness rather. Some players never overcome this weakness, while others, who are perhaps blessed with a very supple and strong wrist, are, with little practice, able to make the backhand stroke with the same dexterity and strength as the forehand. But why would it not be a good idea, when tossing the balls back and forth across the net, as we so often do in practice, to ask the player on the other side of the net to place all the balls on your backhand? Practice that stroke at every opportunity. Use that same easy swing of the arm, of which I have spoken, and you will soon notice an improvement in your backhand play. When I was at college I was once unfortunate enough to break my left arm while skating. With one arm securely bound in splints, life became rather wearisome, and being then even more enthusiastic over Lawn Tennis than I am now, I removed all the pictures from one side of the room which I occupied in a college dormitory, and for an hour at a time practised backhand strokes against the wall. I don't believe that the practise caused my broken bones to knit together any sooner, but what was of more importance, it certainly did improve my backhand stroke. It will pay to practise this stroke as much as possible and improve it, as otherwise a cunning adversary will see your weakness, and place all the balls on your backhand.

A beginner is rarely sufficiently aggressive or

courageous in his game. This is shown in a variety of ways, but most commonly, perhaps, by his disinclination to run to the net when a good opportunity offers; and this is a most serious fault. I suppose that the beginner is apt to fear that if he runs up, his opponent will drive the ball by him. But he should be more courageous. Even if he does once in a while lose a point by running up, he must remember that the advantages to be gained will more than compensate him in the end. He should always bear it in mind, just as if it were a rule of the game, that he must seize every reasonable opportunity to run to the net.

In playing at the net I think that a young player is apt to "smash" *too* much. He is likely to cherish the idea that he is not playing well unless he smashes at everything. Now you will find that the steady and cool men are the ones who win most of the Tennis tournaments. One never saw Sears, who held the championship of this country for seven years, stand at the net and smash as hard as he could at every ball which crossed it. He very often purposely refrained from smashing the ball when he had almost a sure chance, and would rather place it so that his adversary, by hard running, might just reach it, and exhaust himself in the struggle to continue the rally. I do not wish to be understood as advising you never to smash. Smash, and smash hard—for instance, when you are badly in need of one particular point. But instead of using the smash indiscriminately, as so many young players are apt to do, combine with it a certain amount of prudence and care, bearing in mind that the player who at one moment makes a brilliant smash, and at the next knocks the ball into the net or twenty feet out of court, will never be able to beat his steady and careful adversary, although he may be superior to that adversary in actual skill. There is great opportunity for *using* the head when you are playing at the net, and also for *losing* it.

Continuing our search for faults, it seems to me that the beginner or young player is apt to drive too much and toss too little when playing in the back of the court. He seems to be continually hoping and expecting that he *may* drive the ball by the man at the net, and he is willing to hammer away at it with little method and less success, never thinking that it is just as simple and sometimes much more effective to toss the ball over the head of his adversary than to drive it by either side of him. He should drive less and toss more. He should realize that tossing is of great importance, and chiefly so because it gives him an opportunity to run to the net. And so, too, knowing that near the net is the proper place for him to be, as soon as he can safely get there, he should consider driving as of less importance, inasmuch as it does not help him to reach the position at the net.

Again, it is a great mistake, and one very commonly made by old as well as young players, to take too many balls on a half-volley.

There are occasions, it is true, when a half-volley becomes absolutely necessary—when, in fact, the stroke can be made in no other way. But there are many more occasions when the player could easily volley the ball by stepping forward, and he does not do so simply because he yields to the

perhaps natural temptation to make a pretty
stroke. He may make the pretty stroke, but in
nine cases out of ten it will be at the expense of
losing the point, for only a very few of the most
skillful players can half-volley with accuracy.
When the average player attempts it, the chances
are two to one that he has not the faintest idea of
the direction the ball is going to take. It is to a
certain extent a blind stroke, and should be avoided
as much as possible.

It is of the greatest importance to be able to
change your style or method of play occasionally,
in order that you may surprise and worry your
adversary. I doubt if the majority of young
players ever think of this point. They are apt to
have but one method of play, and use it against all
comers; whereas the player who uses his head is
first careful to observe the methods and peculiari-
ties of play of different men, and then attempts to
play a game which may best resist the strong
points of his opponent's method, and most effectively attack its weaknesses. If the player who
"uses his head" thinks that a certain adversary is
apt to become rattled and nervous when compelled
to receive a great many lobs or tosses, then he will
toss and continue to toss until he has rattled him.
But if he knows that that same or some other opponent is particularly strong at smashing, then he
will not toss at all, or certainly as little as possible.
If he commences a tossing game, and finds, after
playing for a time that it is not successful against
a particular adversary, he will not obstinately continue to toss simply because it has been successful
against another, but he will rather change his

method, even in the middle of the set, and try something which may be more effective.

Endurance has now become an important factor in determining the result of a contest at Lawn Tennis. I know of no game, foot-ball not excepted, in which one is so likely to become exhausted or winded as in Lawn Tennis, when the game is hotly contested and played with spirit, as it should be. This being so, some attention should certainly be paid to training and cultivating powers of endurance. It is, of course, especially important to those who play in tournaments, which add so much to the attractiveness of and interest in the game. A hard-fought match of three sets out of five, on a hot summer's day, is a severe test of endurance, and of two men evenly matched in skill, the one who is in the best physical condition will surely win.

A TOURNAMENT AT THE CASINO, NARRAGANSETT PIER, R. I.

CHAPTER VI.

THE DOUBLE GAME.

"So they doubly redoubled strokes upon the foe."
—*Macbeth.*

WHILE there may be some difference of opinion as to whether a contestant in the single game should play at the net or in the back of the court, there can be no doubt as to which is the correct policy in the double or four-handed game. Two players at the net will surely overpower two of equal skill at the base-line, and so it has become the distinctive feature of the modern double game that all four contestants seek to gain positions at the net, where every ball may be volleyed or smashed. In a trial between two teams of unequal strength, one rarely sees all four of the players near the net at the same time, for the stronger two show their superiority by beating back their adversaries toward the base-line, where they have them at their mercy; but when teams of equal experience and skill come together, each resolutely maintains its position, and the repeated crack of the ball against the tightly strung rackets, as it is rapidly volleyed from one to another of the four players, almost reminds one of a volley of musketry. It is the rapidity and swiftness of the strokes which constitutes the charm of the double game, and renders it more attractive for the spectator than a contest in singles.

Even in the old-fashioned double game, the advisability of playing one man at the net was recognized. While one of the two players remained at the base-line the other stood at one side of the court and almost over the net, ready to smash any poorly directed return. This system was then changed to the present, by placing the net man a few feet farther back and advancing his partner, who had formerly played at the base-line, to a point just as near the net. But how near to the net should this point be? This question presents about the only point in contention. Some think that both men should approach as close as possible to the net, while others hold that they should stand as much as ten feet away, where there is less danger that the ball will be driven between them or tossed over their heads. In referring to the single game, it was my opinion that the player should stand nearly midway between the service-line and the net. In the double game I think that both men should be nearer the net, for if the double court (36 feet in width) is divided into two equal parts, each man is obliged to cover a space only 18 feet in width, while the single player must protect his whole court, 27 feet wide. And again, either

partner can easily run to the back of the court
and return a ball which has been tossed over the
other's head. About six or seven feet from the net is
the proper place, in my opinion, and neither partner should approach nearer, except of course to
"kill" or smash.

It is of more importance than one might imagine,
too, that both partners should stand at exactly the
same distance from the net. If a line could be
drawn across the court parallel to the net, each
partner should stand with his feet touching it, for
every step taken by either away from that line
increases the distance between them, and of course
makes a larger hole through which an adversary
may shoot the ball. It follows, then, that when one
player is compelled to move from this imaginary
line, parallel to the net, the other should move also
and in exactly the same direction. If one partner
is forced toward the back of the court, the other
should accompany him step for step. When the
opportunity occurs for a return to the net, the sig-
nal should be given, both should run forward at
one and the same time, and both should stop at
exactly the same distance from the net. Such is
the ideal, the perfect double game; and this line,
this parallel, should never be destroyed, except
when one partner must run forward to smash, or
run back to return a ball which has been tossed
over the other's head.

Up to this point we have been assuming that the
players are in the midst of play or a rally, and we
started by placing them on this parallel line near
the net. But, prior to this, one of the players
must have been serving or receiving a service. Let

us now go back, therefore, and consider the play from the beginning of a game.

Whether your side is serving or receiving the service, the primary idea of yourself and partner must be to reach that line, six feet from the net, and the positions which you assume must be in accordance with that idea. Let us first suppose that you are serving; and right here it is important to consider whether you should serve a very swift or a very slow ball, for the position to be taken by your partner depends upon the decision of this question. In considering the single game, you will remember that there was some doubt as to whether speed in the service was desirable. There is no such doubt in the double game, unless you wish to follow your first service by running to the net, and in that case you should use one of the underhand twist services (Fig. 4, Chap. II.), or the slowest kind of an overhand service. Otherwise it pays to serve with just as much speed as possible, and without thought of economizing strength, in the hope that you may embarrass the striker-out in his return and compel him to give your partner at the net a chance to smash. It has always been my own practice, in playing the double game, to serve my first service as swiftly as possible and to make no immediate attempt to run to the net, for it is almost impossible to recover from the violence of the exertion in time to reach the net before the return. · If my first service is a fault, I always run to the net on the second, taking care to serve so slowly, however, that I can cover the length of the court and reach the net in time to *volley* the return of the striker-out. Some of the best double players, moreover, often prefer to drop the swift service altogether, and to run to the net on a slow first service.

Let us now return to a consideration of the positions to be taken when you are serving. To simplify matters, let us call you and your partner A and B. If A intends to deliver a swift service, B should stand very close to the net and ready to smash, but he must also be careful to completely guard his side of the court. A should serve from a point on the base-line, well over toward the opposite side. If the first service is a fault, B should immediately drop back about six feet and assume a position a little nearer the center of the court than when he stood at the net. He should also take a position similar to that last described, if A intends to make his first service a slow one, or if his swift service is returned without giving a chance to smash. In now serving his slow service, A should remember to direct it toward the center line of the service court, as this allows B to cover more of the court toward the center, and gives A more opportunity to protect his own side as he runs toward the net. When A has arrived at a point where he is just as near the net as B, whether it is six, seven or eight feet, he should stop, and thereafter the movements of both should be made in unison, as before described.

Now let us suppose that one of your adversaries is serving, and that A is to receive the service. If it happens to be one of the slow services, A can stand quite near the service-line to receive it, and should follow his return by immediately running to his position about six feet from the net. B should stand on the other side of the court, about

six or seven feet from the net, while the service is
being delivered, for it is reasonably sure that A
will so return a slow service that your adversaries
will have no chance to smash. But if it happens
that the server has a very severe and speedy service, A must of course stand at or back of the base-
line, and *may* give your adversary at the net a
chance to smash. In this case, therefore, it seems
to me good policy for B to stand as far back as
the service-line, or, perhaps, farther, if the service
is unusually swift; for at that distance from the
net there is some chance that he may be able to
return a smash, while it is practically impossible if
he is only six feet away. As soon as B perceives
that A has returned the service so that there is no
chance for a smash, he should immediately run to
his old position six feet from the net. If the
swift service is a fault, he should likewise advance
toward the net before the second service is delivered.

We have now studied about all of the positions
which A and B are ordinarily called upon to assume during the progress of a game. It is well to
add, however, that while this system of play, which
I have described in such detail, is probably correct
in theory, it will often be upset by any little circumstance out of the ordinary. A general may
carefully map out his campaign, only to find in the
midst of it that some small but unexpected movement of the enemy must cause a temporary change
in his plans. The old ideas are kept firmly in his
mind, however, and every effort is directed toward
a return to the original plan. And so here, while
this system, as mapped out for A and B, may be

temporarily upset, the original idea of gaining the position at the net should be carefully remembered by both men and every effort should be directed toward that end.

In returning a service it is best, as a general rule, to direct the ball toward the server, for he is usually running toward the net, or has just completed the run, while his partner is standing still, alert, and ready to make a return. Assuming that the server is right-handed and that he is serving from the right side of the court, it is also best to direct your return toward the middle of the court, for the server will then be compelled to take the ball on his backhand as he runs toward the net; and if, in addition, you are once in a while successful in driving the ball between the two men, you are doing great work, for there is nothing which can so thoroughly rattle them and disorganize their team work.

But, while these returns are best, as a general rule, it will not do to assume that they should be used continuously, for the main point of a strategic game of Lawn Tennis is to do exactly the opposite of that which your adversary expects. There is naturally more opportunity for such strategy in the single game, where one player is obliged to protect the whole court, 27 feet in width; but even in the double game, a moderate and well-timed variation of play is most effective. A very good illustration of this point is found in the policy which is usually adopted by double players who are well acquainted with the skill of their adversaries. They select that one of the opposing team whom they consider to be the weaker, and make him the target for every shot. But more often than not, it is found that the target is nerved to greater effort by such an attack, and a majority of the points are won by a sudden and quick stroke toward his partner, who is standing idly by and not expecting that he will be called upon to do any of the work. The wisdom of the policy lies not so much in attacking the weakness of one partner, as in surprising the strength of the other.

In my own opinion, the use of any great amount of tossing or lobbing in the double game does more harm than good to the side using it. Many skillful double players, however, will differ with me upon this point. All agree as to the importance of tossing in the single game, but there it is used for at least one purpose, the importance of which is entirely absent in the double game. In singles, endurance is a requisite of success, and the toss or lob is much used for the purpose of winding and weakening an adversary; but men of only average strength may play five or even more sets of doubles with but little effect upon wind or muscle. Only two reasons remain, then, for the use of the toss in the double game: first, because it may enable you to regain the net after you have been driven to the back of the court; and second, because it varies your game and presents an additional element for your adversaries to meet.

These two reasons are good ones, I grant, and justify a moderate or occasional use of the toss, but it must be remembered that there is always one man at the net, and usually two, ready to pounce upon and smash any poorly lobbed ball; not a tired and worn out man, as in the single game, but one with his muscles in good smashing condition. Add to this the fact that the court is 36 feet wide instead of 27, and it is readily seen that the point is almost surely lost, if the chance to smash is given.

I should therefore advise the double player to toss as little as possible. A high toss is much harder to smash than a low one, and the latter should be used rarely, if at all.

It is hardly proper to close this discussion without some reference to the importance of coolness and self-control in the make-up of the double player. All of the circumstances, which annoy the single player and cause him to lose his self-control, are likely to occur in the double game, and, in addition, each partner is continually called upon to exercise the greatest forbearance toward the other. Your partner may have a bad day, may make a series of unfortunate plays, may interfere with your strokes—in fact, may do everything wrong; but you must struggle hard to keep your temper, and do your own share of the work with more skill than ever. If you quarrel and fight among yourselves, you are sure to become rattled, and your adversaries will be encouraged to renewed effort. A cheerful word to the offender, or a laugh, will do more good than a growl. Many of us are able to give only the growl, and we know from experience how much harm it may do.

The following hints, most of which apply to the double game, were clipped from London "Pastime" a few years ago. They may be useful to *some* players, but I should hardly care to recommend them for general adoption:

1. It is easier to call "fault" than to take a fast overhand serv:ce.

2. It is never too late to say you were "not ready."

3. Take *every* ball you can reach with *any* part of your racket.

4. Having rushed at the ball and finding you cannot reach it, shout "yours" to your partner, who is generally to be seen in the most distant corner of the court. Then observe in a reproachful tone, "You know I can't take everything."

5. When in doubt, abuse your partner.

6. Always apologize to everybody about every-thing; it sometimes deceives the spectators into imagining you are capable of better things.

Miss ADELINE K. ROBINSON.

CHAPTER VII.

LAWN TENNIS AS A GAME .FOR WOMEN.*

"Nay, then, I see our wars
Will turn into a peaceful comic sport,
When ladies crave to be encounter d with."
—*King Henry VI.*

IN seeking for exercise and recreation the athletic man has a large field from which to choose his favorite sport. He may play Baseball, Football, Lacrosse, Lawn Tennis, and many other games. How different it is with the athletic woman. She may ride and walk for exercise, it is true; she may row; she may, with perfect propriety, play at mask and foil; but when she tires of these and seeks for a game in which the elements of exercise and competition are combined, Lawn Tennis seems to be her only refuge. It is the one athletic game which a woman can enjoy without being subjected to sundry insinuations of rompishness, and it is de-

* Originally published in "Outing." of July, 1889, and reprinted by permission from that magazine.

cidedly unfortunate for the physical development
of woman that she cannot attain the highest success
even in this, her one sport, without becoming the subject of ill-natured criticism. In the opinion of some
just and impartial critics, the woman who is unfortunate enough to defeat all others "plays just like
a man," "is too ungraceful for anything," etc. But
we of the other sex and, to their credit, the majority
of her own, admire the woman who, for the time being, is unconscious of her personal appearance and
bravely struggles against the awful handicap im-
posed upon her, viz., much dress and little strength.
The physical superiority of the English women to
those of most other nations is well known to be due
to the greater amount of exercise which they take;
and the English girl plays Lawn Tennis much
better than the American simply because she is
physically her superior, and can more easily handle
a racket of adequate weight.

It must be conceded that Lawn Tennis is a game
wonderfully well fitted to be a medium of exercise
for women. It may be played violently or it may
be played gently, entirely at the option of the contestants. Already attractive simply as a game, it
is rendered so much more so by the addition of
tournament playing, that the interest never flags,
but rather increases. And right here lies the
greatest danger. The average male contestant in a
tournament is anxious to win, and willing to exert
himself to a considerable extent to that end, but it
appears to be a feature peculiar to a tournament
for ladies that each and every participant is thoroughly imbued with the idea that she is destined to
win, and the violence of her efforts to avert defeat

causes the game to become a harmful rather than a beneficial exercise. It may be said, somewhat paradoxically perhaps, that Lawn Tennis, although a good game for ladies, is not a "ladies' game," as some sarcastic people were once wont to call it. It is a game which, when too violently played, becomes as severe a strain upon the muscles and produces as serious an effect upon the action of the heart and lungs as any of the most exhausting of athletic sports—a fact which will be attested by any man who has played Lawn Tennis as well as Baseball, Football or Lacrosse.

And now let us consider the equipments which are necessary for the practice of the game. In the first place, what should be the weight and shape of a racket to be used by a woman of ordinary strength? As to shape, popular opinion has now united on the one style, which common sense would dictate to be the correct one: the racket with the straight head, which is now manufactured by almost all of the dealers in tennis goods. But the weight of the racket is an important consideration. A man of ordinary strength should, in the opinion of the most skillful players, use a racket weighing from thirteen and a half to fourteen and a half, or at the most fifteen ounces. The weight to be used by a woman might also in some cases be as high as fourteen ounces, for it is well known that some women have more power in their wrists than the average man, and the wrist plays an important part in the wielding of a racket. It is probable, however, that the correct weight to be used by the woman of ordinary strength is from twelve to thirteen and a half ounces, and it may be asserted positively that she should *not* use a racket of less weight than twelve ounces, for the size and weight of the ball are, of course, uniform, and any racket of less weight than twelve ounces is incapable of resisting and returning a ball propelled with any great degree of force.

The danger of slipping on a smooth turf court and spraining an ankle or a knee is so great, that much care should be exercised in the selection of shoes. It has been found that the ordinary rubber sole will not always prevent slipping, and small steel or iron pegs have been commonly used by men during the past few years. The necessity would appear to be greater in the case of a woman, who labors under the extra disadvantage of having a skirt dangling about her feet. The use of the pegs will very often avert a serious accident and really do no more injury to the turf than the ordinary rubber sole.

As to other items of dress, it is undoubtedly presumptuous for man to advise or suggest. But in view of the statement already made, that Lawn Tennis, when violently played, is most exhausting, it is perhaps pardonable, and certainly pertinent, to quote a paragraph from Dr. Sargent's article on " The Physical Development of Women," which appeared in *Scribner's Magazine* of February, 1889. The paragraph in question reads as follows, and the moral is too plain to be drawn:

"In order to ascertain the influence of tight clothing upon the action of the heart during exercise, a dozen young women consented this summer to run 540 yards in their loose gymnasium garments, and then to run the same distance with corsets on. The running time was 2m. 30s. for each trial, and, in order that there should be no cardiac excitement or depression following the test, the second trial was made the following day. Before beginning the running the average heart impulse was eighty-four beats to the minute; after running the above-named distance the heart impulse was 152 beats to the minute, the average natural waist girth being twenty-five inches. The next day corsets were worn during the exercise, and the average girth of waist was reduced to twenty-four inches. The same distance was run in the same time by all, and immediately afterward the average heart impulse was found to be 168 beats per minute. When I state that I should feel myself justified in advising an athlete not to enter a running or rowing race whose heart impulse was 160 beats per minute after a little exercise, even though there were not the slightest evidence of disease, one can form some idea of the wear and tear on this important organ, and the physiological loss entailed upon the system in women who force it to labor half their lives under such a disadvantage as the tight corset imposes."

When we begin our practise of the game, our first thought, of course, is of how to improve in skill. It is true that many appear to be perfectly satisfied with batting the ball back and forth across the net with as little exertion as possible, but the natural impulse of the American, whether man or woman, is to reach the highest degree of excellence in whatever he or she undertakes. In considering improvement in Lawn Tennis, the first thought which occurs to the mind is that woman, as compared with man, labors under at least two serious disadvantages—first, her manner of dress, and, second, her lack of muscle, endurance or lung power and other qualities, all of which we will unite and call by one term—strength.

Her disadvantages, then, are manner of dress and lack of strength, and in seeking to improve, it must be her aim to make these disadvantages of as little effect as possible. It is obvious that the wearing of a long and flowing skirt not only seriously interferes with quick movements from one part of the court to another, but what is of still more importance, it prevents a woman from using her racket and making the stroke in a correct manner, or, as it is more commonly called, in "good form." There is a right way and a wrong way to make a Lawn Tennis stroke, just as there is a correct method and incorrect method of using a bat in baseball or cricket. A baseball player is taught by the master of good form that he must meet the ball squarely, with his bat held in a horizontal position, while the cricketer is instructed that he must guard his wicket by holding and using his bat in a perpendicular line; and so, in order to play in "good form," the Lawn Tennis player, in returning the ball from a bound, must make the stroke with the arm in as nearly a perpendicular line as possible, and not with the round-arm movement so commonly seen. To be more explicit, the player must station himself or herself sufficiently far back to meet the ball on its descent from the bound, assuming, of course, that there is time to take that position, and the stroke should be made when the ball has nearly reached the ground for a second

time, the arm then being stretched to its full length
and moving freely in a line parallel with the body
(Chapter III., page 37).

It being conceded that the stroke just described
is the correct one, both from a scientific and common sense point of view, it is easy to see that a
woman is seriously embarrassed in adopting the
correct method, for if she attempt to make the
stroke with her arm close to and parallel with her
body, the chances are about even that either the
ball or her racket will become entangled in, or at
least interfered with by, the folds of her skirt. In
fact, it is quite impossible for her to make a stroke
in the manner described. Now can anything be
done to overcome this disadvantage? The most
obvious remedy that suggests itself is that she
should take a less number of balls on the bound,
or, in other words, that she should learn to volley.
Volleying is a feature of Lawn Tennis which perhaps no women, or certainly very few of them,
appear to have mastered, and the one who first
attains proficiency in this branch of the game will
have a decided advantage over her opponents. To
volley well requires strength, a lack of which is
one of the two disadvantages under which woman
labors; but, on the other hand, is it not sometimes
a saving of strength if one can run to the net and
by one well-directed volley put an end to a rally
which may be prolonged to an almost indefinite
length, if each contestant remains in the back of
the court and takes ball after ball on the bound?
Such protracted rallies are terribly exhausting, and
any woman who has the strength to endure them
must also have strength enough to volley well.

Many devotees of Lawn Tennis will remember with much pleasure the numerous exciting matches between Miss Robinson and Miss Roosevelt during the summer of 1888. In some of these, notably the Narragansett Pier Tournament, there were rallies in which the ball crossed the net more times than in any contest between men which I have witnessed. The sight was of course a pretty one, and it was the kind of playing sure to provoke unlimited enthusiasm among the spectators; but as an expert Lawn Tennis player watched the ball fly back and forth across the net time after time, he could not but feel an inclination to step into the court, run to the net, and with one vigorous "smash" put an end to the exhaustive rally.

If it be once granted that volleying requires no more strength than is necessary to endure these long rallies, there is no reason why a woman should not learn to volley with skill and precision, and when she has once mastered that art she will very seldom be annoyed by her manner of dress.

It may be doubted that women can attain proficiency in that branch of volleying which we call "smashing the ball," and yet there is no unanswerable reason why she should not. A "smash" may be made by exerting the strength of the whole arm or that of the wrist. Thomas Pettitt, the well-known professional player, almost invariably "smashes" by a mere movement of the wrist, and there is no lack of power in his "smashes." In addition to being a much more graceful stroke, it is more deceptive than a "smash" in which the whole arm is used, for an adversary is less likely to know where you intend to place the ball. It

is well known that some women are blessed with
wrists of steel, and that the wrists of the majority
of the sex are of much more power, as compared
with those of men, than other parts of the body.
It does not seem impossible, then, that a woman
should be able to "smash," and "smash" effectively,
too.

But can she learn to "smash," volley, and play
all of the other difficult strokes of Lawn Tennis
without sacrificing a certain amount of grace?
The question is a serious one, for if women become
imbued with the idea that they must lose the grace
natural to their sex and take on the awkwardness
of man, in the same proportion that they show improvement or approach perfection in the game, it
would be difficult to persuade them to take that
active interest which is always inspired by a desire
to excel in any sport, and Lawn Tennis would be
deprived of that feature which has distinctly
marked it as the most refined and unprofessional
of all athletic games. Fortunately the question
may fairly be answered in the affirmative.

It is the universal desire of Lawn Tennis players
to play in "good form." It is hard to give a defi-
nition of "good form," but one of its chief requi-
sites is to give a free and easy swing to the arm in
making a stroke. To play in "good form" means
to play gracefully, for grace is necessary to "good
form." It is very seldom that one sees a beginner
in Lawn Tennis who does not make the strokes
with his arm cramped and stiffened. He plays in
"bad form," and it is only after long experience
and practice that he acquires the easy movements
necessary to "good form." And so a woman, who

in the first attempts is even more awkward than a
man, will find that her movements will become
more easy and graceful the more that she plays
and the more that she learns of the game, while
the very confidence which proceeds from a con-
sciousness of one's improvement in skill is often an
important element of grace.

There is one stroke in which the gentler sex
plainly excels, and that is "lobbing" or "tossing."
The explanation probably lies in the fact that the
stroke is itself a gentle one, requiring delicacy and
deftness, rather than strength, for its proper execution. I have seldom seen any lobbing by expert
men players which would compare in effectiveness
with that of Miss Robinson or Miss Roosevelt in
some of the matches in doubles which they played
during the summer of 1888. It was in doubles
that they were allowed the greatest opportunity
for an exhibition of such skill, for in their single
matches each contestant almost uniformly played
in the back of the court, and the "lob" or "toss"
is used only when an opponent is playing at the
net. The importance of this stroke is often under-
estimated by men, who would find their playing
much improved if they used it more often, or were
able to make it with greater skill.

The fact that a woman can probably "lob" or
"toss" with a skill equal to that of an expert man
would seem to operate as an argument against the
advice already given, viz., that she should learn to
volley and play at the net, for if a ball is tossed
over her head it is much more difficult for her to
turn quickly and run to the back of the court, and
it might be pleaded in addition that her limited

powers of endurance would not always be sufficient
to stand the strain. To this it may be answered
that the position at the net is considered by the
most experienced players to be such a commanding
one, and of such vital importance to success, that
it is worth incurring almost any risk to secure it.
The ball may often be tossed over your head, just
as it may frequently be driven down one of the side
lines; but it is believed that, in spite of such re-
verses, more is to be gained in the end by sturdily
maintaining your stand at the net and awaiting a
good opportunity to "kill" the ball.

It can hardly be stated with perfect fairness that
the future of Lawn Tennis is certain. It is comparatively a new game, although evolved from a
succession of old ones, and while it has made more
progress during the past few years, so far as number and enthusiasm of followers are concerned,
than any other game, it is not yet certain that it
will endure the test of time, or that it will not
prove to be one of those games which enjoy popular favor for a decade and then become almost
a reminiscence. Many will remember the time
when Croquet had its thousands of players, and
almost every lawn was laid out with stakes and
wickets. Now the resounding thwack of the Croquet mallet and ball is no longer heard in the land.
The game is still played, it is true, but as a popular pastime it has long faded from public view. It
is hardly fair to compare Lawn Tennis with Croquet, for, although the latter possesses many agree-
able features, it is not sufficiently active to be
called an athletic game and used as a sole medium
of exercise, nor will an impartial critic hold that it

possesses the merit of Lawn Tennis, when viewed purely as a means of amusement. It is unquestionable, however, that the athletic world is fickle; it has an enormous appetite for novelty, and each successive generation, as a matter of *course*, desires to be served with a new kind of game. And so it is possible that Lawn Tennis may some time lose the place it now holds in popular favor. It is at present protected by one very important circumstance, which exists in the fact that here is a game which man and woman alike may enjoy as a pastime and employ as a means of recreation. Let Lawn Tennis retain the active interest of the fair sex, and there is every reason to believe that it is assured a great and an abiding popularity.

PART II.

THE GAME AS IT *HAS BEEN* PLAYED.

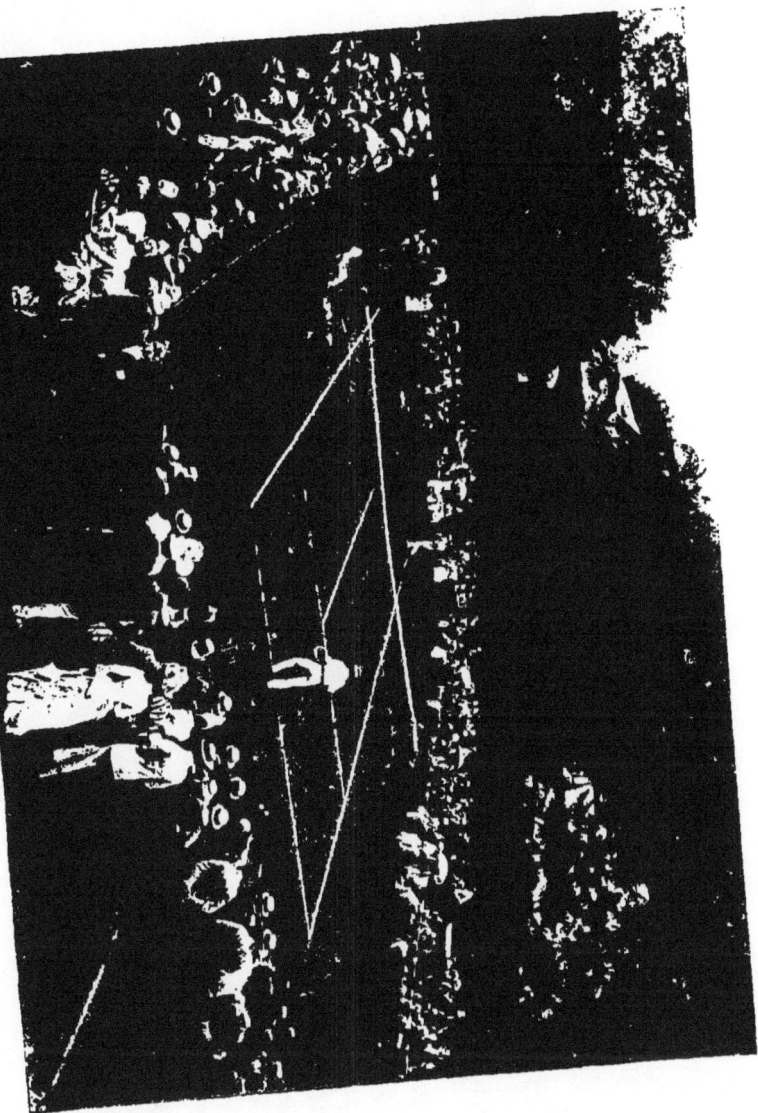

CHAMPIONSHIP MATCH, NEWPORT CASINO, AUGUST 30, 1887.
(FROM A PHOTOGRAPH BY ALMAN.)

CHAPTER I.

THE INTRODUCTION AND EARLY HISTORY
OF THE GAME.

TENNIS and Lawn Tennis are two games which are not infrequently confused. The former is played in an indoor court of special and complicated construction. The surrounding walls are joined together at various angles, and the floor, upon which the players stand, is marked with a number of lines, which are called chaces. This is the game which was played hundreds of years ago, a fact which is established by the references of many noted writers. Shakespeare, for instance, puts the following metaphor in the mouth of King Henry V., upon the occasion of his receiving a present of some tennis balls from the Dauphin:

> "When we have match'd our rackets to these balls,
> We will, in France, by God's grace, play a set
> Shall strike his father's crown into the hazard.
> Tell him he hath made a match with such a wrangler,
> That all the courts of France shall be disturb'd
> With chaces."

These lines are evidence, not only that Tennis must have been widely played in both England and France during that period, but also that it was a game well entitled to be called "the sport of kings."

It is this confusion of the two games which has led some to believe that Lawn Tennis is an ancient game. Lawn Tennis is undoubtedly a product or an evolution of those ancient sports, such as Tennis and Rackets, but the game itself is distinctly modern. It was the first game of that class (unless the comparatively unimportant sport called Battledore and Shuttlecock be considered) which was played out of doors, and it was for that reason, more than any other, that it became immediately so popular and widely played.

The game attracted very little attention in the United States, however, until about 1880, and at that time but few people were aware of the fact that in the neighborhood of Boston it had been actively and, all things considered, skilfully played since 1874. In view of the frequent assertions that the game was not introduced in this country until 1878 or 1879, it may be interesting to know exactly when and by whom the first set of Lawn Tennis was imported from England.

After careful investigation, it seems to be well established that the distinction belongs to a gentleman of Boston, who purchased the set in England, more as a curiosity than anything else, and brought it to this country in the summer of 1874. The court was laid out and the set was first used at Nahant, a summer resort a few miles from Boston, in the month of August, 1874. The rackets were awkward in shape, and much lighter than those

now in use; the balls were of uncovered rubber,
similar to the toy balls with which children play,
and the net was about five feet in height. Dr.
James Dwight and Mr. F. R. Sears, Jr., were the
first to use these crude materials, and those gentlemen were undoubtedly the pioneers of the game
in the United States. Dr. Dwight has since become
famous as a player, both at home and abroad, but Mr.
Sears abandoned the game before it had become at
all widely known. He was an elder brother of Mr.
R. D. Sears, well known as the champion of the
United States for seven successive years, and who
has often said that his elder brother would have
been a better player than himself had he not been
obliged to discontinue practice at such an early
day. It is possible that there was a large streak of
Lawn Tennis in the Sears blood, but it is more likely
that the skill afterwards shown by Mr. R. D. Sears
was due to the instruction of his brother and Dr.
Dwight, and to his observance of their methods.

Some time in the summer of 1874, another set
was brought to this country by Mr. W. W. Sherman,
of Newport, but it was not until the following spring
that a court was laid out. It was in the summer of
1875, therefore, that the game was first played at
Newport, a city which has since been the scene of
many memorable encounters.

The two courts already mentioned were laid out
on private grounds, and it remained for the Staten
Island Cricket and Base Ball Club to first adopt
Lawn Tennis as a club sport. Mr. E. H. Outerbridge, of Staten Island, was the fortunate possessor
of a set, and also a prominent member of the Staten
Island Club. A number of Englishmen, who were

more or less familiar with the game in their own country, were also members and eager to play. Mr. Outerbridge therefore obtained the permission of the club authorities, in the summer of 1875, to plant his Lawn Tennis seed in a modest corner of the grounds. That the seed sprouted and the plant thrived will be demonstrated by a visit to the grounds of this same club on any afternoon of the summer months.

It is quite safe to assume that numerous matches were played both at Staten Island and Nahant in the summer of 1875, but no accurate records can be found, as the newspapers then paid no attention to the sport. In 1876, however, we have an authentic record of the first tournament played in the United States. It was a local affair, held on a private court at Nahant, and as Dr. Dwight and Mr. F. R. Sears, Jr., were plainly superior to the remainder of the players, it became necessary to make it a handicap. The scoring was done according to the method employed in Rackets, each player serving until he lost a point, and fifteen points constituting a game. It was quite common for a good player, after winning the toss for service, to serve out the game, scoring fifteen points in succession. Dr. Dwight and Mr. Sears were of course placed at scratch, and the remaining thirteen contestants were allowed large handicaps. Dr. Dwight won the tournament, but only after the hardest kind of a battle with Mr. Sears.

The following year, 1877, saw a repetition of this local handicap. This time Mr. F. R. Sears, Jr. did not compete, but the tournament is particularly interesting to us inasmuch as it was the occasion for

the first appearance of Mr. R. D. Sears, then a boy
of fifteen years. It is recorded that R. D. Sears
was allowed a handicap of eleven points by Dr.
Dwight, and was defeated by a score of fifteen
points to eleven, or in other words, the future
champion failed to score a point, while Dr. Dwight
was rolling up fifteen. Nine points were conceded
to Mr. A. L. Rives, and this was the smallest handicap allowed by Dr. Dwight, who was, of course,
again placed at scratch. Mr. Rives is the same
gentleman whose name will be found among the
contestants in the · championship tournaments
played at Newport in 1888 and 1889. It is perhaps
unnecessary to add that Dr. Dwight won this
handicap even more easily than the one of the
year previous.

Still another tournament was played at Nahant
in the following summer, 1878, and it was interesting for several reasons. For the first time the present
method of scoring, which had previously been used
only in Court Tennis, was adopted. It was once
more a handicap, and Dr. Dwight was placed at
scratch, but this time not alone. Two players,
Messrs. Shaw and Peabody, appear to have been
considered worthy to be classed with the redoubt-
able Doctor, but inasmuch as he succeeded in defeating both, there seems to be no reason for doubt-
ing that he was then the most skillful player of our
own country. It would be too much to say, however, that he had no superior in the United States,
for it is more than probable that there were several
visiting Englishmen who had learned enough of
the game in their own country to enable them to
concede odds to our best players.

But the most interesting feature of the 1878 tournament, at least to players of the present time, was the opportunity it afforded for another comparison of the playing merits of Dr. Dwight and Mr. R. D. Sears. The Doctor conceded to his pupil odds of thirty and three bisques, and in addition gave him a sound beating. For the benefit of those who are unfamiliar with the value of bisques, it may be said that a handicap of thirty and three bisques amounts in value to considerably more than half forty. It can readily be seen, then, that during the year 1878 the embryo champion was so far behind his teacher that the pursuit must have seemed hopeless.

We have no record of any events of importance occurring during the year 1879, but it is nevertheless certain that Lawn Tennis must have taken a long stride forward in popular favor, for at the very beginning of the following year, interest in the game, which had before been confined to a few, now became general. Many were disposed to ridicule the sport as one suitable only for women and weak men, and the rougher element were more or less prone to jeer at the white flannel trousers and knickerbockers, but when the strongest athletes among the Cricketers and Base Ball players found something in the game to amuse them, the jeers and sneers were in a measure silenced.

The press, too, about this time began to pay some attention to the new game, but treated it rather as a freak of fashion or a successor to Croquet, which had been extremely popular, but was then dying a rather rapid death. Some of the articles which appeared in the daily newspapers must be very amusing to the players of to-day. The following is a fair sample of the Lawn Tennis journalism of those times. It is a quotation from an article published in a Philadelphia paper, and refers to a tournament which was played at least a year later than the time which we are now considering, but it indicates very plainly that the knowledge of the press and the general public, upon the subject of Lawn Tennis, must have been extremely slight during this whole period:

"Fine weather having made it possible for the devotees of the fashionable diversion of Lawn Tennis to adjourn from indoor practice to the enlarged freedom of out-of-door participation in the game, the sport has just begun to blossom out in full favor, and, as a sort of inauguration of the season, a "tournament" of skilled players took place yesterday near Wayne Junction, at "Stenton," the picturesque grounds of the Young America Cricket Club. There were two kinds of sets played, the "single," in which one man on each side of the net fought the balls of the other, and the "double," in which were two players on each side. All the players wore Tennis suits, some of them with brightly striped jackets and caps, and more entirely of white, while the majority wore tight fitting knee breeches and long colored stockings. . . . In the drawings, Lindley Johnson drew a "bye," so that he did not participate in the single games. The playing in all these games was very pretty. Van Rensselaer's performances were occasionally beautiful, and he was most dexterous throughout, although Thayer, his competitor, excels him in grace. Dr. Dwight has a rolling sailor's gait, and a sort of grocer's sugar-scoop dip with his racket, but when he touches the ball it seems to obey his will, and goes irresistibly back to where it came from. His playing won the admiration of all. Especially in the difficult matter of "serving" the ball to his adversary, he displayed the very highest qualities requisite to the best playing of the game."

But notwithstanding all this, Lawn Tennis was destined to prosper. Until the year 1880, all tournaments and matches had been local affairs similar to those which have been mentioned as occurring at Nahant. Consequently players in one part of the country were entirely unfamiliar, not only with the skill of those living in another section, but also with the rules, etc., which governed their play. The Young America Cricket Club, of Philadelphia, had taken to the game with enthusiasm; the members of the Staten Island Cricket and Base Ball Club were playing it more and more, and Dr. Dwight and Mr. Sears had a host of followers in the neighborhood of Boston. In each of these localities, however, the play was governed by rules which differed widely in some important particulars. Each club had a kind of "go as you please" method of its own. It is not surprising, then, that the first meeting of the representative players of the country produced some confusion and quite a little feeling.

Early in the summer of 1880, the Staten Island Cricket and Base Ball Club threw open its gates for the first open tournament held in the United States. Any player in the country was privileged to enter, and the winner was to be declared the Champion of America. Both singles and doubles were played. The singles were won by Mr. O. E. Woodhouse, a celebrated English player, who happened to be in New York at this time. Although Mr. Woodhouse was then, without doubt, by far the best player in the United States, it would be hardly proper to award him the title of champion for the year 1880, inasmuch as other tournaments were given by various clubs during the same summer and each was declared to be for the champion-ship.

It was the double event, however, which had the greatest effect upon the development of Lawn Tennis in this country, for it was marked by a disagreement which plainly showed the necessity of a central power or body, which should frame a code of rules to be used by all players alike. Messrs. Dwight and Sears were entered in the doubles, and upon their arrival from Boston, found that the balls which were used in the tournament play were not more than two-thirds of the size of an English ball, which they had continually used in practice, and to which they were thoroughly accustomed. The two balls also differed materially in weight. The Boston men protested that the tournament balls were not regulation, either in weight or size, but the tournament committee answered by pointing to the word "Regulation," which was stamped in bold letters upon the balls. Dwight and Sears were therefore obliged to play with the balls which were offered, or not play at all. They chose the former alternative, and were easily defeated by a New Jersey team, Messrs. Wood and Maning. The experience was valuable, however, for it constituted the first step toward the formation of the United States National Lawn Tennis Association.

A short time after the events just mentioned, a tournament was held at Newport, R. I. It was a local affair, the entries being limited to members of the Casino, but it attracted attention to the advantages of the place, and led to its being selected for the championship meeting of the National Association in the following year.

It was in the autumn of 1880, however, that a match was played, which materially hastened the formation of an association. The Young America Cricket Club, of Philadelphia, having quite a number of expert players among its members, decided to challenge the Staten Island Cricket and Base Ball Club to play a four-handed match. The challenge was accepted, and the match was played at Philadelphia. The Young America Club was represented by Mr. C. M. Clark, an elder brother of Mr. J. S. Clark, and Mr. F. W. Taylor, whose name is still seen among the entries in the championship tournaments at Newport. The Staten Island team, Messrs. J. S. Rankine and W. M. Donald, won the match, but only after a desperate contest.

The result would have been unsatisfactory, however, no matter which side had gained the victory, for the ball question again provoked a dispute, and the matter was further complicated by a difference of opinion in regard to the proper height of the net. The Philadelphia men had taken all of their practice with the net at a height of three feet and six inches at the center, while the Staten Islanders were accustomed to a net measuring three feet at the center and three feet and six inches at the ends. A difference of six inches at the center of the net was perhaps of more importance then than it would be at the present day; at least it would so appear from a consideration of the style of play then in vogue.

During all these years it had been customary for the players, in both the single and four-handed games, to stand at the back of the court, in the neighborhood of the base line, and receive every ball on the bound. Such a thing as running to the net was unheard of, at least in the single game, and any good volleying was so rare as to cause an exclamation of astonishment from an adversary, and profound admiration from a spectator. Lobbing or tossing, as practised at the present time, was unknown, for no one played at the net, and there was therefore no occasion for any such art. The theory of their game was to drive the ball swiftly, and at the same time close to the top of the net. But the nets which were used generally throughout the country, except at Staten Island, and possibly at Boston, measured four feet in height at the ends, and it was difficult to send a ball with much speed over four feet of net, and still cause it to fall within the lines, especially since the player of those days had no knowledge of the scientific drop stroke, which is now used so effectively. It was only natural, then, that a majority of the returns were directed toward the center of the net, where it measured only three feet and six inches. It follows, too, that a difference of six inches at the center was decidedly material, and the discussion which had arisen between the Staten Island and the Philadelphia players was bound to be renewed so long as there was no central power which had the authority to determine the proper height of the net, and settle other matters then in dispute.

But all of these tournaments and matches, which were played during 1880, had attracted the attention of many who had hitherto been indifferent to the game. The formation of an Association was earnestly urged by the prominent players, foremost

among whom was Dr. Dwight, and finally a call for
a general meeting was issued in the names of the
following: The Beacon Park Athletic Association
of Boston, the Staten Island Cricket and Base Ball
Club of New York, and the All Philadelphia Lawn
Tennis Committee, the latter being composed of
representatives of all prominent Cricket clubs of
Philadelphia. The meeting was held at the Fifth
Avenue Hotel, in New York City, on the 21st of
May, 1881. As many as thirty-three Clubs were
represented. A Constitution and By-laws for an
Association, to be called the United States National
Lawn Tennis Association, were adopted, and Mr.
R. S. Oliver, of the Albany Lawn Tennis Club,
was chosen as the first President. Mr. C. M. Clark
was elected Secretary and Treasurer, and three
other gentlemen were selected, who, together with
the officers, were to constitute an Executive Committee. The matters in dispute during the previous year were thoroughly discussed, and it was
decided to adopt the rules of the Marylebone
Cricket Club and the All England Lawn Tennis
Club for the ensuing year. It has since been the
policy of the Association, in the exercise of its
power to make, revise and interpret the playing
rules, to follow the English rules except in a very
few instances where it was manifest that a change
would improve the game.

The Association also voted to hold a championship tournament during the summer, the winners
in both the Singles and Doubles to be called the
champions of the United States. The Executive
Committee afterwards met and agreed that these
championships should be decided at Newport, R. I.

The English ball made by Ayres was adopted as the regulation ball to be used in the United States. The power and authority of the National Association was at once recognized throughout the country, and the very commencement of its career was marked by a prosperity which has since been uninterrupted.

CHAPTER II.

THE CHAMPIONSHIPS OF THE U. S. N. L. T. A.

SINGLES.

DURING the spring and early summer of 1881, an interesting series of matches, most important in their effect upon the style of play then in vogue, were played by Messrs. Dwight and Sears. Mr. Sears had been rapidly improving in skill during the previous year, and at its end was in close rivalry with Dr. Dwight for the honor of being considered the best native player. The Doctor, however, still remained slightly the better. Just before play was resumed in the spring of 1881, Mr. Sears, in casting about for ways and means to get the better of his rival, determined to try the experiment of playing at the service line, instead of at the base line, as described in the last chapter. The change was a radical one, for in the old game nearly every ball was taken on the bound, while playing at the service line required that practically all of the returns

Howard Augs Taylor

should be volleyed or half-volleyed. But greatly to
Mr. Sears' surprise, upon his first meeting with Dr.
Dwight, he found that the Doctor had also conceived
the same idea and adopted the same style of play.
The two men then practiced the new game continually, but their volleying bore little resemblance to
that of the present time, for it amounted to little
more than tapping the balls back and forth. Nor
would either of these gentlemen wish to be understood as claiming the honor of the invention of the
volleying or net game, but it is worthy of note that
this important element of play was not, like the rest
of the game, an importation from England, but the
product of the thought of two of our own players.
It is an interesting fact, too, that while Englishmen
had been familiar with the art of volleying for some
time, this very year was the first in which W. Renshaw won the championship of England, and his
victory was mainly secured by continually running
to the service line and swiftly volleying every return.

That the adoption of the service line game by Mr.
Sears must have had a tremendous effect upon play
in this country will be seen, when we come to con-
sider the first championship tournament of the U. S.
N. L. T. A., which was begun on the 31st day of
August,

1881.

No better place than the Newport Casino could
have been selected. The grounds were picturesque
and the courts well kept. The accommodations for
the players were good, and Newport being then, as
now, a very fashionable resort, the most beautiful

women of the country graced the tournament with their presence.

Both Singles and Doubles were played, but as it was afterwards decided to sever the two events and play the Doubles at some place other than Newport, making practically a separate tournament of each, it is perhaps best to treat them as separate from the beginning, and confine the present chapter to a description of the play in Singles.

All of the then prominent players of the country were entered, with the exception of Dr. Dwight, whose ill health allowed him to compete only in the Doubles. Boston was represented by Messrs. R. D. Sears, Shaw and Gray. Philadelphia provided the largest number of contestants, Messrs. Van Rensselaer, Newbold, C. M. Clark, F. W. Taylor and others entering from that city, but the first named playing only in the Doubles. Messrs. Conover and Miller appeared for the State of New Jersey, Messrs. Nightingale and Smith came from Providence, and Mr. W. E. Glyn represented not only the Staten Island Club, but also the English element.

The tournament was undoubtedly one of the most interesting ever played in this country, but an instantaneous photograph of some of the scenes would appear strange and amusing to the players of the present day. The scoring was done by the present method, but all matches, until the final, were the best two out of three sets, with none deuce and vantage. Mr. Sears and a few others used a service, which was a poor imitation of the present overhand method, but the remainder of the contestants never thought of attempting anything more than a plain

1st Round.	2d Round.	3d Round.	4th Round.	Final Round.
Sears, 6-0, 6-2.	Sears, 6-1, 6-2.	Sears,		
Powell.	Anderson.			
Gammell, 1-6, 6-3, 6-1.		6-3, 6-5.	Sears,	
Newbold.				
Glyn, 1-6, 6-1, 6-1.	Glyn, 6-5, 6-2.	Nightin- gale.		
Rives.	Conover.			
Conover, 6-1, 6-1.			6-3, 6-0.	Sears.
Morse.				
Rathbone, 6-5, 5-6, 6-5.	Shaw, 6-3, 6-5.	Shaw,		
Saunders.	Rathbone,			
Gray, 6-5, 6-3.		4-6, 6-3, 6-1.	Gray.	
Hines.				
Nightingale, 6-2, 6-0.	Nightingale, 6-4, 6-3.	Kessler.		
Caldwell.	Barnes.			
Anderson, 6-2, 6-0.				Champion,
Randolph.				R. D. Sears,
Barnes, 6-2, 1-6, 6-1.	Gray, 6-0, 6-0.	Glyn,		6-0, 6-3, 6-2.
Miller.	Coggswell.			
Coggswell, 6-4, 6 5.		6-4, 4-6, 6-4.	Glyn,	
Congdon.				
Smith, by default.	Kessler, 6-1, 6-2.	Gammell.		Glyn.
Eldridge.	Smith.		6-2, 6-2.	
Kessler, 6-1, 6-4.				
Pruyn.				
Shaw, a bye.	Gammell, a bye.	Gray, a bye.	Shaw.	

SCORE OF THE CHAMPIONSHIP TOURNAMENT OF 1881.

NEWPORT, AUGUST 31ST.

(DRAWING BY OLD SYSTEM.)

In this and the following scores the winner of each match is printed in heavy faced type.

underhand cut. The courts were in very good condition, but the Executive Committee apparently did not consider it objectionable to decide a match in Singles upon a court marked out for Double play, as this was continually done. The contestants, with a single exception, played the base line game, and that exception was Mr. Sears, who continued his volleying tactics at the service line. The others were unfamiliar with this style of play, and each one, who was drawn against the Boston man, seemed impelled, as if by a magnet, to direct every return across the centre of the net, and straight into the hands of Mr. Sears, who calmly tapped first to one side of the court and then to the other, and thus won the first championship of the United States with scarcely an effort. The racket used by Mr. Sears weighed sixteen ounces, and was much too heavy for ordinary play, but not for his purpose, which was merely to block or stop the ball. The harder his despairing adversaries drove the ball against the heavy racket, the harder it went back. Lobbing or tossing was then unknown, and he was therefore relieved from the greatest danger to which his style of play could have been subjected. His closest match was with Mr. Nightingale, in the third round, while the final against Mr. Glyn was almost a walk over. And thus the medal, offered by the Association as an emblem of the Championship of the United States, for the year 1881, was won by Mr. R. D. Sears, of Boston, without losing a single set.

But although Mr. Sears had worthily won the title, he was obliged, for the time being, to forego the honor of being considered the best player in the

Godfrey M. Brinley -

United States. Immediately after the decision of the
championships, a new tournament in Singles was
arranged, of which it was one of the conditions that
the entry list should be open to any player, whether
a member of the National Association or not. The
chief object of this competition was to bring together
Mr. Sears and Mr. J. J. Cairnes, an Englishman,
who was then at Newport, but who had been debarred from competing in the National tournament.
A handsome prize, known as the Ladies' Cup, was
offered to the winner. There were many entries,
more, in fact, than for the championship tournament,
but the issue finally narrowed down to Mr. Sears and
Mr. Cairnes, just as had been desired. It will be
remembered by those who were present that the at-
mospheric conditions of the day, upon which these
two players met to contest the final match, were so
peculiar as to attract the general attention of scientific men. It was afterwards known throughout New
England as the "Yellow Day." Mr. Sears did not
play in quite his usual form, but it is certain that he
was then no match for the Englishman, who won in
three straight sets, and thereby captured the Ladies'
Cup.

1882.

The successful tournament of the previous year
had now increased the interest in Lawn Tennis to a
wonderful degree, and the meeting held by the Association in the spring of 1882 was an enthusiastic
one. No changes in the rules were made, but Dr.
Dwight was elected president in place of Mr. Oliver.
The second championship tournament was begun at
Newport on the 30th day of August, and the rapid

1st Round.	2d Round.	3d Round.	4th Round.	5th Round.	Final R'd.
Thorne, 6-4, 6-1.	Smith, 6-2. 6-2.	Conover 2-6,6-0,6-2,			
Newbold.	Le Roy.	Thorne.	Sears,		
Rathbone 6-0, 1-6, 6-4.	Kneeland by default.	J. S. Clark, 6-3, 6-0.	6-1, 6-4.	Sears,	C. M. Clark,
Paton.	Van Rensselaer.	Baillie.	Conover.	6-0, 6-4.	
Codman, 6-3, 6-3.	Conover, 6-2, 6 3.	Powell, 6-0, 6-1.			6-3, 6-2.
Benson.	Butler.	Rathbone	Rankine,	Rankine.	Sears.
Powell, 6-5, 4-6, 6-3.	Baillie, 6-1, 6-0.	Sears, 6-1, 6-4.	6-4,5-6,7-5,		
Woodman.	Metcalf.	Glyn.	Powell.	Gray.	
Dwight, 6-1,6-0.	Sears, 6-4, 6-1.	C. M. Clark.			
Boardman.	Johnson.	6-5, 6-1.	C. M. Clark,	C. M. Clark,	
Nightingale, by default.	Gray, by default.	Codman. Nightingale, 6-4, 6-1.	6-3.2-6,6-1.	withdrawn.	Champion. R. D. Sears. 6-1, 6 4, 6-0.
Draper.	Agassiz.	Eldridge.	Rives.		
Rives, 6-1, 6-0.	Malcolmson, 1-6, 6-1, 6 3.	Rives, 4-6,6-1,6-5,		Dwight	
Thomes.	Brooks.	Kneeland	Gray,		
Rankine, 6-4, 3-6, 6-1.	Glyn, 6-2, 6-0.	Gray, 6-1, 6-1,	6-4, 6-4.		Sears, a bye.	C. M. Clark.
Miller.	Hynes.	Smith.	Nightingale.		
Allen, 6-4, 5-6, 6-2.	J. S. Clark 6-5, 6-1.	Dwight, withdrawn.		Sears, a bye.	
Carryl.	Post.	Allen.	Dwight, 6-1, 6 0.	Gray, a bye.	
	Clark, 6-3, 6-1.	Rankine, 6-0, 6-0.	J.S.Clark		
	Boit.	Malcolmson.			
	Eldridge, by default.				
	Roby.				

SCORE OF THE CHAMPIONSHIP TOURNAMENT OF 1882,

NEWPORT, AUGUST 30TH.

growth of the game was shown by the forty entries
in the Singles, against twenty-five in the previous
year. Among the new comers were Mr. J. S. Clark,
then a student at Harvard, and Mr. E. Thorne, a
Yale man. The former has since played a conspic-
uous part in Lawn Tennis history, but Mr. Thorne
made his first and only appearance in this tournament, a fact much to be regretted, for, although a
beginner, his volleying was so severe and so true
that practice would have made him one of the foremost players of the country.

All of the old players were again on hand, and this
time Dr. Dwight had entered, but those who had
looked forward with pleasure to a meeting between
him and Mr. Sears were again disappointed, for after
easily defeating J. S. Clark in the third round, the
Doctor sprained an ankle, while playing his first set
against Mr. C. M. Clark, and withdrew. Mr. Clark
had a slight lead at the time and the issue of the
match was decidedly doubtful.

The general style of play was materially different
from that of the year before. Every player served
an overhand service, and nearly every one of the
forty entries, all of whom had played the base-line
game in 1881, now became an imitator of Mr. Sears,
and rushed to the net at every opportunity. But the
champion had the advantage of a year's start at this
game. His volleying no longer consisted of tapping
or blocking the ball. It was now so accurate and
severe, that he was easily superior to the others, and
repeated his performance of the previous year, by
winning the championship without losing a set.
Surprise has often been expressed that Mr. Sears

was able to retain the championship for so long a period, as he afterwards did, and this tournament of 1882 seems to provide a very fair explanation of his remarkable superiority. Just as he was then a year ahead of his fellow players in the art of volleying, so did he always afterwards remain a year ahead of them in all the finer points of the game. If a new stroke was developed, such as the drop stroke, for instance, he was always the first to introduce it into this country, but not until he himself had thoroughly practiced it and become almost perfect in its execution. When, together with this fact, it is considered that he had a natural aptitude for athletic sports in general, it is not so difficult to understand and account for his brilliant record.

After Dr. Dwight withdrew from this tournament, it became a foregone conclusion that Mr. C. M. Clark would meet Mr. Sears in the finals. No one had been able to win more than five games in two sets against Mr. Sears, and Mr. Clark was able to secure only the same number in the three sets which composed the final match. Mr. Sears was therefore hailed as champion for a second time, and while a few still considered Dr. Dwight his equal, the great majority believed him to be clearly the best player in the United States at the end of the year 1882.

1883.

There was no legislation of importance at the next meeting of the Association, and Dr. Dwight was re-elected president. The third championship tournament was begun on the 21st of August. Many of the oldest and most skillful players were not entered. The Clark brothers were abroad, trying to capture

1st Round.	2d Round.	3d Round.	4th Round.	Final Round.
W. B. Dixon, 4-6, 6-3, 6-1.				
L. Bonsal.	Dwight,			
A. Newbold, by default.	6-3, 6-0.	Dwight.		
G. W. Beals.	Paton.			
II. W. II. Powell, 6-2, 6-0.		6-2, 6-3.		
—. Wharton.	Sears,	Brinley.	Sears,	
R. F. Conover, 5-6, 6-1, 6-1.	6-1, 6-4.			Sears.
J. Tooker.	Farnum.		6-0, 6-0.	
G. M. Brinley, 6-5, 6-1.				
H. Hooper.	Smith,	Sears,	Keene.	
M. Paton, 6-5, 6-4.	6-5, 6-1.	6-2, 6-0.		
W. F. Metcalfe.	Eldridge.			
G. M. Smith, by default.		Powell.		Champion, R. D. Sears. 6-2, 6-0, 9-7.
—. Williams.	Brinley,			
W. II. Bucknall, 6-5, 6-5,	6-4, 5-6, 6-3.			
W. Gammell, Jr.	Newbold.			
M. Post, 6-4, 6-4.		Keene,		
J. H. Powell.	Conover,	6-3, 6-4.		
J. Dwight, 6-0, 6-2.	6-2, 6-2.		Dwight,	
M. Thomes.	Dixon.	Smith.		
F. Keene, 6-4, 6-1.			6-4, 6-3.	
—. Johnson.	Keene,			Dwight.
F. Eldridge, 6-5, 3-6, 6-4.	6-2, 6-4.		Conover.	
F. J. Hynes.	Post.	Conover,		
C. Farnum, 6-2, 4-6, 6-4.		a bye.		
H. A. Taylor.	Powell,			
R. D. Sears, a bye.	6-1, 6-5.			
	Bucknall.			

SCORE OF THE CHAMPIONSHIP TOURNAMENT OF 1883,

NEWPORT, AUGUST 21st to 24th.

English laurels, and Mr. Glyn and Mr. Nightingale were unable to play. New life was infused into the game, however, by the entries of several of the younger generation of players, and notable among these were G. M. Brinley, Foxhall Keene, Charles Farnum and H. A. Taylor, the last named being the same player whose record has since been so brilliant. But no one was considered to have any real chance for the championship except Mr. Conover, Dr. Dwight and Mr. Sears. The two ancient rivals from Boston met in the final round, as expected, and a deuce and vantage set was then played for the first time at Newport. Mr. Sears really won an easy victory, but the third and final set was extremely close, the score being 9-7. By finally winning this set and match, the popular champion completed a most wonderful record, having played through three championship tournaments without losing a single set.

The methods of play shown in this tournament differed but little from those of the year previous, although a general improvement was noticed. Shortly afterwards, Messrs. Dwight and Sears went abroad to enjoy the winter Tennis in the south of France, and neither of these gentlemen was present at the next convention of the Association, held in New York during the early months of
1884.

One very important step was now taken. It was resolved that the champion should be debarred from competing in the All-Comers tournament, and required to defend his title against the winner, who should challenge him immediately upon the termination of the contest. The interest in the next tour-

Preliminary Round.	1st Round.	2d Round.	3d Round.	4th Round.	Final Round.

```
R.L.Beeck-      R. L. Beeck-
 man,            man,
 6-3, 6-2.       6-5, 6-1.        Beeckman,
M. Post.        S. H. Hooper.    1-6, 6-5, 6-2.    Beeck-
W. V. S.         P. Willis,                         man,
 Thorne,         6-3, 6-3.        Willis.
 6-0, 6-1.      A. L Rives.                         6-1, 6-2,
F. Warren.      W. P. Knapp,                                     Knapp,
G. M. Brin-      6-4, 6-2.        Knapp,
 ley,           F. H. Gillette.   6-1, 6-1.        Knapp.
 6-5, 6-1.      W. E. Eaton,
W. Merriman      by default,      Eaton.
                J. Dwight.
                H. A. Taylor,
                 6-1, 6-1.        Taylor,                        6-2,2-6,6-1.  Taylor.
                Brinley.          3-6, 6-2, 7-5.   Taylor,
                J. S. Clark.      J. S. Clark.
                 6-2, 6-0,                         6-4, 6-1.
                W. F. Metcalfe.                                  Taylor.
                A. Van
                Rensselaer,       Van Rens-
                 6-5, 6-1.        selaer,          Van
                W. H. Barnes.                      Rensse-
                R.F.Conover       6-4, 2-6, 6-3.   laer.
                 6-2, 6-2.        Conover.
                F. Keene.                                        Winner,
                —. Thorne,                                       H. A. Taylor,
                 0-6, 6-5, 6-4.   Thorne,                        6-4, 4-6, 6-1, 6-4.
                M. Paton.
                H. W.             by default,      Thorne,
                Slocum, Jr.       Slocum.
                 4-5, 6-2, 6-3.                    by
                F. J. Hynes.                       default.      Thorne,
                G. Richards,      Richards,
                by default.       4-6, 6-5, 6-4.   Richards.
                —. Wood.
                E. Butler,        Butler.
                 6-2, 6-1.
                W. V. R. Berry.                                  2-6,6-2-6-3.   Thorne.
                C. M. Clark,      C.M.Clark,
                 6-3, 6-4.        6-4, 6-1.        C. M.
                —. Curtis.        Lyman.           Clark,
                P. Lyman,
                 6-3, 6-3.                         6-2, 6-2.     C. M.
                —. Halliwell.                                    Clark.
                —. Galt,          Galt,
                 6-5, 6-1.        6-4, 6-1.        Galt.
                E. Denniston.                                    Championship,
                M. Fielding,      Fielding.                      R. D. Sears,
                 6-1, 6-4.                                       6-0, 1-6, 6-0, 6-2.
                W. Gam-                                          H. A. Taylor.
                mell, Jr.
```

SCORE OF THE CHAMPIONSHIP TOURNAMENT OF 1884,

NEWPORT, AUGUST 26TH TO 30TH.

(DRAWING BY BAGNALL-WILD SYSTEM.)

nament, which was played during the last week of
August, was much enhanced by the adoption of this
rule. With Mr. Sears entered, the result would have
been a foregone conclusion. With him out, it was
an open question. Dwight and Sears returned from
abroad just before the tournament, and the former
entered, but did not play in the Singles, although
his game had been vastly improved by practice with
English experts. The Clark brothers reappeared,
however, and now, for the first time, more or less
college feeling crept into the competition, for W. P.
Knapp and W. V. S. Thorne, under-graduates of
Yale, were pitted against H. A. Taylor and J. S.
Clark, of Harvard. R. L. Beeckman and H. W.
Slocum, Jr., a Yale graduate, also made their first
appearances, the former being then a most promis-
ing and the latter a very inferior player.

This tournament of 1884 was chiefly remarkable
for the brilliant performance of H. A. Taylor, then
only 17, or at the most 18 years of age. Veterans
and new comers alike went down before him. He
defeated Brinley, J. S. Clark, Van Rensselaer, and
finally the two Yale men, Knapp and Thorne, in
rapid succession. He was the smallest in stature of
all the players, and no one who witnessed it will for-
get his plucky fight against the veteran giant, Van
Rensselaer. But while giving full credit to Mr.
Taylor, it is only just to add that one, whom he defeated early in the tournament, was probably his
equal in skill. Mr. J. S. Clark was at this time in
his best form. He was drawn against Mr. Taylor in
the second round, won the first set, lost the second
and was within one point of winning the third and
the match. If he had succeeded in scoring that one

R. Livingston Beckman

last point, it is almost certain that J. S. Clark would have been recorded as the winner of the All-Comers Tournament of 1884 instead of H. A. Taylor.

Immediately after winning, Mr. Taylor of course challenged Mr. Sears for the championship. This match calls for little comment, inasmuch as the champion, fresh from practice with the best players of England, had no difficulty in retaining his title. Mr. Taylor deserves credit, however, for capturing one set, a feat which no one up to this time had been able to accomplish.

1885.

This year was marked by a large amount of Lawn Tennis legislation. In the first place, the playing rules were amended to conform as far as possible to those used in England. A contrary move was made, however, in respect to the ball. Up to this time, the English ball, manufactured by Ayres, had been universally used, but now certain members of the Association, moved by patriotism and sundry other causes, made a successful effort to secure the adoption of a ball manufactured by a New York firm. This ball afterwards turned out to be an utter failure.

This was the year, also, in which a new challenge cup was offered by the Association. The cup was emblematic of the championship, and it was necessary to win it in three not necessarily consecutive years, before it became the property of the holder. Another step in the right direction was taken, by resolving that all sets in the All-Comers Tournament should be deuce and vantage.

The annual tournament was played at Newport in the month of August, as usual, and for the first time, no one of those veteran players, who had supported

Preliminary Round.	1st Round.	2d Round.	3d Round.	Final Round.
R. L. Beeckman, 6-1, 6-2.	J. S. Clark, 6-2, 1-6, 8-6. Beeckman.	Clark,		
G. A. Smith.		7-5, 1-6, 6-3.	Clark,	
H. Lilienthal, by default.	A. Moffat, 6-0, 9-11, 6-3.	Moffat.		
C. M. Clark.	Mansfield.			
F. S. Mansfield, 6-3, 6-3.			6-4, 6-3.	Knapp,
C. E. Garrett.	Knapp, 6-0, 6-2.	Knapp,		
W. P. Knapp, 6-1, 7-5,	Hooper.			
W. Shippen.		4-6, 10-8, 6-2.	Knapp.	
—. Nightingale, 6-3, 4-6, 7-5,	H. A. Taylor, 6-4, 6-2.	Taylor.		
H. S. Morgan,	Nightingale.			
C. B. Davis, 6-3, 7-5.				Winner, G. M. Brinley 6-3, 6-3, 3-6, 6-4.
P. E. Presbrey.	G. M. Brinley, 6-1, 4-6, 6-2.	Brinley,		
S. H. Hooper, 9-7, 6-2.	H. W. Slocum, Jr.		Brinley.	
F. J. Hines,		6-2, 6-1.		
F. Keene, 9-7, 6-2,	Davis, 6-1, 6-0,	Davis.		
F. H. Gillett.	Lillienthal.			
W. V. R. Berry, 6-3, 6-1.			3-6, 9-7, 6-1.	Brinley.
M. A. DeW. Howe.	Berry, 6-3, 2-6, 6-3.	Berry.		
F. Warren, 3-6, 6-3, 7-5.	Warren.		Berry.	Championship, R. D. Sears, 6-3, 4-6, 6-0, 6-3, G. M. Brinley.
W. Lewis.	Keene, by default.	6-2, 6-1.		
	M. Paton.	Keene.		

SCORE OF THE CHAMPIONSHIP TOURNAMENT OF 1885.

NEWPORT, AUGUST 18TH TO 21ST.

the game in its earlier days, was present. The familiar names of Dwight, C. M. Clark, Conover and Van Rensselaer did not appear in the entry list of the tournament. All these had dropped out one by one, leaving the field to the younger generation of players, such as J. S. Clark, Beeckman, H. A. Taylor, Brinley, Knapp, Thorne and Slocum. Much to the surprise of a great many, the All-Comers was won by G. M. Brinley, of Trinity College, a left-handed player of remarkable dash, grace and brilliancy. His narrow escape from defeat in the third round, at the hands of Mr. W. V. R. Berry, is worthy of note. Mr. Berry had won the most important tournaments of the summer, and the judgment of those who thought that he could easily defeat Mr. Brinley, was apparently confirmed when he won the first set and rolled up a score of five games to one in the second. Mr. Brinley's chance of winning the All-Comers here hung by a slender thread, but a succession of brilliant plays suddenly turned the scale in his favor and finally enabled him to win the match.

This tournament was indeed a succession of surprises. Two of these were furnished by Knapp, the Yale champion, who defeated both of his Harvard rivals, H. A. Taylor and J. S. Clark. Knapp thus earned the right to play against Brinley in the final round, but was rather easily defeated.

The championship match was the old story over again. Since the meeting of 1884, Mr. Sears had made another trip to England and returned to this country with an entirely new stroke. It was the famous drop stroke, which by some chance was misnamed in the United States, and became generally known as the " Lawford. " Sears used it with tell-

ing effect in his match with Brinley, and easily won
the championship of the United States for the fifth
consecutive time.

1886.

The American ball had proved so unsatisfactory,
that it was now thrown out and the Ayres ball re-
adopted. It was thought that a match of two out of
three sets afforded an unsatisfactory test of the relative merits of two players, and it was therefore determined that three out of five sets should constitute
a match in all future championship tournaments.
Only the odd or deciding set should be deuce and
vantage, except in the final round. The adoption of
this rule naturally made endurance an element of
much more importance than before.

Dr. Dwight had again been abroad, but returned
during the summer and determined to try for the
championship once more. He therefore entered the
All-Comers, which was begun at Newport, as usual,
on the 23d day of August. The luck of the drawing
brought together Dr. Dwight and H. A. Taylor in
the preliminary round, and their meeting produced
one of the hardest contests ever fought at Newport.
Dwight's chief trouble was his lack of endurance,
and after easily winning the first two sets, he was
obliged to succumb to his plucky adversary in each
of the next three, the fifth and deciding set being
won by the remarkable score of 13–11, and that, too,
after the Doctor had been several times within one
point of winning it.

A number of very young players appeared at Newport for the first time in this tournament. Among
these were Mr. O. S. Campbell, who made a good
fight against Mr. Slocum in the first round ; the

Preliminary Round.	1st Round.	2d Round.	3d Round.	4th Round.	Final Round.
P. E. Presbrey, 6-3,6-1,6-5. Gamble.	Presbrey, 6-2. 3-6, 6-2, 6-4. G. M. Brinley. J. S. Clark; 6-0, 6-1, 6-1. Edgar.	Brinley. 6-0,6-4,6-3. Clark.	Clark. 1-6.6-5 6-5, 6-2.	Clark,	
W. H. Barnes. 6-4,2-6,6-3, 4-6,6-4. G. A. Smith.	H. W. Slocum, Jr. 4-6, 6-1, 6-3, 6-0, O. S. Campbell. P. S. Sears, 5-6,4-6,6-1,6-0,6-3. W. R. Weeden.	Slocum, 6-2,4-6.6-2, 4-6,6-3. P. S. Sears.	Slocum.		
	H. A. Taylor, 0-6,3-6,6-1,6-2, 13-11. J. Dwight. W. V. R. Berry, 6-4,5-6,4-6,6-4,6-1. G. McKenzie.	Taylor. 6-0,6-0.6-1. Berry.	Taylor,	6-5,6-2,6-3.	Taylor.
			Taylor, 6-3,6-5.6-5.	Taylor.	
	Q. A. Shaw, Jr. 6-4, 6-4, 6-0. W. Gammell, Jr. Smith, 6-1, 6-1, 6-0. Manice.	Shaw, 6-0,6-1,4-6, 6-1. Smith.	Shaw.		
	R. L. Beeckman, 6-0, 6-0, 6-1. Miller. H. M. Sears. 2-6,6-3,6-3,5-6,7-5. Nightingale.	Beeck- man. 6-2,6-0,6 0. H. M. Sears.	Beeck- man. 6-4.3 6 6-0, 6-3.	Beeck- man,	Winner. R. L. Beeckman. 2-6,6-3.6-4,6-2.
	F. S. Mansfield, 6-1, 6-0, 6-0. W. Lewis. M. Fielding. 6-2, 6-2, 6-3. S. H. Hooper.	Mans- field, 6-4,6-1,6-3, Fielding.	Mans- field.	Beeck- man.	
	C. A. Chase, 6-0, 6-3, 6-0. A. L. Rives. Robbins, by default. d'Invilliers.	Chase, 6-5,6-3,6-2. Robbins.	Chase, 6-0,6-2.6-4.	Chase.	
	M. Post, by default. M. Paton. F. Warren, 7-9,2-6,6-3.6-0,6-4. F. W. Taylor.	Post, 6-2,6-4,3-6, 2-6,6-2. Warren.	Post.	Championship, R. D. Sears. 4-6, 6-1, 6-3, 6-4. R. L. Beeckman.	

SCORE OF THE CHAMPIONSHIP TOURNAMENT OF 1886,

NEWPORT, AUGUST 23D TO 28TH.

Sears twins, brothers of the champion, and Mr. Q. A. Shaw, Jr., also from Boston. Mr. C. A. Chase, the champion of the West, also made his first attempt to win championship honors in the East.

Brinley, the All-Comers winner of the previous year, was badly beaten by J. S. Clark, who also disposed of Slocum's chances in a close contest. Taylor, in the meantime, had continued to play in the same brilliant form which he had shown against Dwight, and after defeating Clark, it seemed almost certain that the honor of meeting the champion should once more fall to him. A serious obstacle arose, however, in the person of Mr. R. L. Beeckman, of New York. This player had been continually improving in skill and was exactly " on edge " when he met Taylor in the final round. The contest was close and a pretty one, but the swift and effective drop stroke of Beeckman won the day.

The championship match which followed was most exciting, for Mr. Sears suffered a much nearer approach to defeat than ever before. When Beeckman won the first set, it was quite generally believed that the champion's unbroken series of victories had come to an end. He pulled himself together, however, and by a violent effort won the next three sets. It is said that Dr. Sears was not in the best of form at the time of this match, but it is only just to concede to Mr. Beeckman the honor of being the first player of this country who was able to force the unconquerable Sears to exert himself to the utmost in a championship match.

It may be interesting to note the relative positions of the experts at the end of the year 1886. A player, who was familiar with the abilities of each, ranked

Quincy Alex. Shaw.

them as follows : 1, Sears ; 2, Dwight ; 3, Beeckman ; 4, Taylor ; 5, Clark ; 6, Slocum ; 7, Brinley ;
8, Mansfield ; 9, Moffatt ; 10, Conover.

1887.

At the next meeting of the Association, held in
March, it was determined to make still another
change in the ball.   The ball manufactured by
Wright & Ditson, of Boston, was adopted as Regulation, and gave almost universal satisfaction.   Mr.
R. D. Sears was elected president of the Association,
the membership of which had been more than
doubled since the organization in 1881.   About sev-
enty clubs now sent delegates to the annual convention.

As the time for the All-Comers again drew near,
there was considerable speculation as to the result of
the championship, for it seemed to be generally believed that a few of the first-class players were approaching nearer than ever before to the standard
of excellence set up by Mr. Sears.   Mr. Beeckman
and Mr. Slocum were looked upon as the most likely
winners of the tournament, and the fortunes of war
brought them together in the first round.   Mr.
Slocum won after four hard fought sets.   No new
player showed skill sufficient to attract much attention, but there was some interest in the debut of
young Mr. Fearing, of Newport, and Mr. W. L.
Thacher, a new Yale champion, won a place in the
third round by defeating Brinley.   Slocum won from
Clark in the third round, and thus earned the right
to play H. A. Taylor in the final.   This match was
a desperate one, Slocum winning in three remark-
ably close sets.

The idea that the other players were gaining on

Preliminary Round.	1st Round.	2d Round.	3d Round.	Final Round.
Q. A. Shaw, Jr. by default, A. E. Wright. W. Cushman. 12-10, 5-7, 6-1, 6-3.	F. Mansfield, 6-2, 8-6, 6-1. H. C. Bowers. J. N. Clark, 8-6, 6-3, 8-6. Q. A. Shaw, Jr.	Mansfield, 3-6, 6-2, 6-8, 6-1, 6-4. Clark.	Clark,	
W. K. Thacher, H.C. Bowers, by default, W. R. Weeden.	G. R. Fearing, Jr. 8-6,3-6,6-4,6-1. C. E. Garrett. H. W. Slocum, Jr.	Fearing,	6-8, 6-4, 6-3, 6-2.	Slocum,
M. Fielding. 6-4, 6-4, 6-0. R. L. Beeckman,	6-2, 4-6, 9-7, 6 3. R. L. Beeckman.	6-1, 7-5, 6-2. Slocum.	Slocum.	Winner, H. W. Slocum, Jr. 12-10, 7-5, 6-4.
O. S. Campbell. 6-3, 6-2, 7-5. H. A. Taylor.	Ganson Depew 6-1, 6-4, 6-3. H. A. Taylor.	Taylor, 6-1, 1-6, 6-3, 6-1.	Taylor,	
H. Emmons, 6-1, 6-4, 6-1. W. H. Barnes.	F. Warren. 6-3, 6-2, 6-0. P. S. Sears.	Sears.	6-3, 6-1, 6-1.	Taylor.
G.R. Fearing, Jr. 6-4, 6-4, 6-0. W. Lewis.	G. M. Brinley, 6-4, 6-1, 6-2. H. Emmons.	Brinley, 6-4, 8-6, 3-6, 6-4.	Thacher.	
P. Manchester. 6-0, 6-2, 6-0. C. E. Garrett.	F. W. Taylor. 6-3, 9-7, 6-3. W. K. Thacher.	Thacher.		Championship, R. D. Sears, 6-1, 6-3, 6-2. H. W. Slocum, Jr.

SCORE OF THE CHAMPIONSHIP TOURNAMENT OF 1887.

NEWPORT, AUGUST 22D TO 30TH.

the champion was apparently exploded, when Mr.
Sears defeated Mr. Slocum for the championship with
seeming ease. This victory was an important one
for many reasons. Mr. Sears had now won the challenge cup for the third time, and it therefore became
his personal property. It will be remembered, too,
that Mr. Renshaw had first captured the championship of England in 1881, the same year in which Mr.
Sears had first won the honor in this country. Both
men had succeeded in retaining their titles until this
year, when a physical injury had compelled Mr. Renshaw to lose by default. This victory of 1887 therefore gave Mr. Sears a lead of one year over Mr. Renshaw.

It is a singular coincidence that our champion was
afterwards compelled, like Mr. Renshaw, to withdraw from the competition on account of an injury.
All interested in the game sincerely hope that the
withdrawal is only temporary and that the victories
of the future will be even more numerous than those
of the past, but it is quite possible that the championship match of 1887 brought the Lawn Tennis career
of this wonderful player to a fitting end. It completed
a record of victories, not marred by a single defeat.

A study of the Newport matches played by Mr.
Sears discloses some interesting facts. During the
seven years in which he held the championship,
or from 1881 to 1887, inclusive, he played eighteen
matches in Singles and won them all. Those eighteen
matches were composed altogether of forty-six sets,
of which Mr. Sears won forty-three. Of those forty-
three, twelve were love sets, and in eight others the
score was 6-1. Mr. Sears won in all 270 games,
against 101 won by his adversaries.

1888.

When it became certain, during the early part of this year, that Mr. Sears' injury would necessitate his retirement, each of the expert players practiced with renewed zeal, in the hope that the mantle of the champion would fall upon his shoulders. Even the veteran Dwight determined to try once more, and therefore sent in his entry for the All-Comers tournament in August. C. A. Chase, J. A. Ryerson, Emerson Tuttle and B. B. Lamb were welcomed as representatives of the Western players, while the East furnished its usual quota.

Chase and Slocum were drawn together in the preliminary round, and although the latter won, he played in such miserable form that there was apparently no chance of his winning the tournament. Mr. P. S. Sears, brother of the champion, made a strong fight to retain the championship honors in his family, but was compelled to succumb to H. A. Taylor, who was playing his usual admirable game. His victory over Mr. P. S. Sears carried Mr. Taylor into the final round in company with Mr. Slocum, who had taken a decided brace and defeated Clark, Dwight and Campbell in rapid succession. The final match between Taylor and Slocum was decidedly uninteresting, the former going to pieces and allowing his rival to win easily. Mr. R. D. Sears then made his default in the championship match, and H. W. Slocum, Jr. became champion for the year 1888, as well as the first holder of the new challenge cup which had been offered by the Association.

There was considerable diversity of opinion as to the relative merits of the various players who ap-

Preliminary Round.	1st Round.	2d Round.	3d Round.	4th Round.	Final Round.
H. W. Slocum, Jr. 5-7, 6-2, 1-6, 6-2, 6-3 C. A. Chase.	Slocum, 6-2, 6-0, 6-0. W.H.Barnes. J. S. Clark. 6-3, 3-6, 6-1, 6-2. F. L. V. Hoppin.	Slocum, 6-2, 6-3, 6-2 Clark.	Slocum,		
	J. Dwight, 6-3, 6-1, 6 2. F. W. Taylor. C. E. Stickney, by default. E. Tuttle.	Dwight, 6-1, 6-0, 6-1 Tuttle.	Dwight.	4-6, 6-3, 6-0, 6-2. Slocum, 6-2, 6-3, 6-4.	Slocum,
	C. Beatty, 6-3, 6-3, 9-7. C. P. Wilbur W. Waller, 7-5, 6-3, 6-2. O. S. Campbell.	Wilbur, 6-2, 6-1, 6-3. Campbell.	Campbell,		
	F. Warren, 6-1, 6-2, 6-3. M. Fielding A. E. Wright. 6-2, 6-3, 6-3.	Fielding, 2-6, 6-2, 6-1, 6-1. Wright.	Wright.	4-6, 6-3, 1-6, 8-6, 6-2. Campbell	
	J.F.Brown,Jr. W. R.Weeden 6-4, 7-5, 6-2. G. W. Lee. W. L. Jennings, 6-2, 6-3, 6-2.	Lee, 6-2, 6-0, 6-1. Sears.	Sears,		Winner, H. W. Slocum, Jr. 6-4, 6-1, 6-0.
	P. S. Sears. A. Hubbard, 8-6, 6-3, 3-6, 6-0. J. A. Ryerson, A. L. Rives. 6-1, 6 2 6-1.	Ryerson 6-2, 6-0, 3-6, 11-9. Lamb.	Ryerson.	8 6, 6-0, 6-4. Sears, 5-7, 6-4, 6-2, 6-2.	Taylor.
	B. B. Lamb H. A. Taylor, by default. F.A.Kellogg. G.M. Brinley, by default. R. B. Hale, P. E. Presbrey.	Taylor, 6-1, 6-1, 6-1. Hale.	Taylor,		
	19-21, 8-6, 6-1, 3 6, 6-4. T. S. Tailer. A. L. Williston. 6-4, 6-8, 7-5, 3-6, 6-2. V. G. Hall.	Presbrey, 2-6, 6-4, 6-4, 6-4. Williston.	Williston	6-2, 6-3, 7-5. Taylor.	Championship, H. W. Slocum, Jr. by default. R. D. Sears.

SCORE OF THE CHAMPIONSHIP TOURNAMENT OF 1888,

NEWPORT, AUGUST 20TH TO 25TH.

peared during this year. The following ranking
was published over the signature of H. A. Taylor :
1, Slocum ; 2, Taylor ; 3 Dwight ; 4, Clark ; 5,
Chase ; 6, P. S. Sears ; 7, McMullen ; 8, Campbell ;
9, Beeckman ; 10, Mansfield ; 11, Shaw ; 12, Hall ;
13, Wright ; 14, Williston ; 15, Hobart.

1889.

The next convention of the Association elected
J. S. Clark to the presidency. There was no other
legislation of importance, but the year 1889 will always be remembered by Lawn Tennis players with
much interest. For the first time an international
flavor was given to the competition at Newport by
the appearance, as a contestant, of Mr. E. G. Meers,
an Englishman who had ranked among the first ten
men of his own country during the previous year.
Foreign competitors we had had before, to be sure,
but this was the first time that one had come with
the avowed purpose of capturing our championship.

The All-Comers was begun on Wednesday, the
21st of August. Mr. Meers was successful until the
fourth round, when, strange to say, it fell to the lot
of one of our youngest players to dispose of his
chances. Mr. O. S. Campbell had been gradually
improving until he had earned a place among the
foremost players, but in this particular tournament
he surpassed himself, for he had already excited
surprise by defeating the two veterans, J. S. Clark
and H. A. Taylor, before meeting Mr. Meers in the
fourth round. By far the best feature of Campbell's
play was his volleying, and he now used it against
the base line game of the Englishman with such excellent judgment and skill, that the latter was com-

1st Round.	2d Round.	3d Round.	4th Round.	Final Round.
C. A. Chase, 6-0, 6-3, 6-1.	Chase, 6-4, 6-0, 6-3.	Chase, 6-4,6-4,4-6,6-3.	Shaw,	
F. O. Reade. A. L. Rives, 6-2, 6-2, 6-1.	Hale.			
R. B. Hale, F. W. Taylor, 6-2, 6-2, 8-6.	Beach, 7-9, 6-2, 6-0, 6-2.	Shaw.		
R. V. Beach. Q. A. Shaw, 7-9, 7-5, 6-3, 6-4.	Shaw.			Q. A. Shaw, Jr.
A. E. Wright. J. A. Ryerson, 6-0, 5-7, 6-0, 7-5.	Ryerson, 7-5, 8-6, 6-2.	Knapp, 6-4, 6-3, 6-2.	4-6,6-1,6-4, 6-4.	
A. L. Williston. W. P. Knapp, 6-2, 8-6, 4-6, 6-2.	Knapp.		Knapp.	
M. Fielding. Deane Miller, 6-4, 8-6, 6-1.	Miller, 6-2, 6-2, 6-3.	Miller.		
R. C. Sands. G. R. Fearing, Jr. 6-3, 6-2, 6-4.	Fearing.			Winner, Q. A. Shaw. Jr. 1-6,6-4,6-3,6-4.
W. W. Reese. F. L. V. Hoppin, 6-3, 6-0, 6-1.	Hoppin, 7-5, 6-0, 6-1.	Mansfield, 6-1, 6-2, 6-2.	Meers,	
S. C. Fox. T. S. Tailer, 9-7, 6-0, 6-1.	Mansfield.			
F. S. Mansfield. E. W. Gould, Jr. 6-3, 6-0, 6-2.	Wright, 7-5, 6-3, 6-4.	Meers.		
M. R. Wright. E. G. Meers, 6-4, 6-3, 6-3.	Meers.		5-7,6-1,5-7, 6-4, 6-2.	O. S. Campbell
C. F. Sands. G. A. Hurd, 8-6, 6-4, 2 6, 6-4.	Chase, 2-6, 6-1, 0-6, 6-4, 7-5.	Clark, 10-12, 7-5, 6-3, 6-3.	Campbell.	
S. T. Chase. J. S. Clark, 6-3, 7-5, 6-4.	Clark.			
W. R. Weeden. H. A. Taylor, 6 3, 6-3, 6-0.	Taylor, 6-4,6-4,5-7,6-2.	Campbell.	Championship, H. W. Slocum, Jr. 6 3, 6-1, 4-6, 6 2. Q. A. Shaw, Jr.	
R. P. Huntington, Jr. O. S. Campbell, 6-4, 6 1, 6 2.	Campbell.			
F. A. Thomson.				

SCORE OF THE CHAMPIONSHIP TOURNAMENT OF 1889.

NEWPORT, AUGUST 21st TO 28TH.

pelled to lower his colors and resign all claim to
the championship of the United States.

But Mr. Campbell was not the only young player
to win honors in 1889. Mr. Q. A. Shaw, Jr., of
Boston, had likewise taken a mighty stride forward.
Mr. P. S. Sears being abroad, the hopes of the Bostonians were centered upon Mr. Shaw, and the re-
sponsibility must have nerved him to greater effort,
for, after disposing of Chase, the Western champion,
he met and rather easily defeated W. P. Knapp, a
veteran player, who now reappeared after an absence
of three years. This latter victory carried him into
the final round, where he met Campbell, fresh from
his conquest of the Englishman. The two young
players fought it out with determination, but the
terrible drives of the left-handed Shaw proved too
much for Campbell and gained the day for Boston.

For some reason or other, Mr. Shaw failed to continue his excellent work in the championship round
and was easily defeated by Mr. Slocum. The latter
therefore became champion for a second time.

Each year it becomes more and more difficult to
properly place the various players in order of
merit. The following list is perhaps as fair as any:
1, Slocum; 2, Shaw; 3, Campbell; 4, Taylor; 5, Chase;
6, Clark ; 7, Knapp ; 8, R. P. Huntington, Jr.; 9,
P. S. Sears ; 10, Mansfield. Of the ten men named,
it is noticeable that every one, except the last, is a
college man, either graduate or undergraduate.
Shaw, Taylor, Clark and Sears are Harvard men,
Campbell belongs to Columbia, Chase to Amherst,
and Slocum, Knapp and Huntington owe allegiance
to Yale. The last named is an undergraduate, who

may well be proud of his first year's record. His numerous successes, together with those of Shaw and Campbell, will cause 1889 always to be remembered as the young players' year.

The following table gives in concise form the results of the championship tournaments, which have been played at Newport from 1881 to 1889, inclusive :

SINGLES CHAMPIONSHIPS.

YEAR.	CHAMPION.	ALL-COMERS, WINNER.	RUNNER-UP.
1881	R. D. Sears.	———	W. E. Glyn.
1882	R. D. Sears.	———	C. M. Clark.
1883	R. D. Sears.	———	J. Dwight.
1884	R. D. Sears.	H. A. Taylor.	W. V. S. Thorne.
1885	R. D. Sears.	G. M. Brinley.	W. P. Knapp.
1886	R. D. Sears.	R. L. Beeckman.	H. A. Taylor.
1887	R. D. Sears.	H. W. Slocum, Jr.	H. A. Taylor.
1888	H. W. Slocum, Jr.	H. W. Slocum, Jr.	H. A. Taylor.
1889	H. W. Slocum, Jr.	Q. A. Shaw, Jr.	O. S. Campbell.

A study of the above table is very interesting. The year 1884 was the first in which the holder of the championship was debarred from competing in the All-Comers tournament, and inasmuch as Mr. Sears, until that year, had been compelled to play through the tournament, he should in equity be given the credit for winning three All-Comers. Mr. H. W. Slocum, Jr. is credited with two, while no other player has won more than one. On the other hand, the record of Mr. H. A. Taylor is the most consistent (always excepting that of Mr. Sears) of any of those whose names appear in the table. Mr. Taylor won the All-Comers in 1884, since when his name appears in the table in every year except two, 1885 and 1889, and even in those years he occupied the sixth and fourth positions among the expert players of the country.

It is somewhat remarkable that the name of J. S. Clark, who has played since 1882, and who at one time was the most prominent rival of Mr. Sears for first honors, does not anywhere appear in the above record.

It is also worthy of note that a majority, or three of the five men, who have won the All-Comers, are left-handed players. The three are Messrs. Taylor, Brinley and Shaw. This fact is the more remarkable when it is considered, that these three men are the only left-handed players whom the writer can remember as having competed at Newport during the past six years. Yet each has achieved this high honor in Lawn Tennis. Does it not suggest the idea that the left-handed man is naturally more adept in the use of a racket? There is certainly an ease of movement, a free swing of the arm, a freedom of action generally, which is characteristic not only of the three players named, but in fact of almost all left-handed men who attempt this game.

The college element is again largely represented in the above record. Both of the champions, every winner of the All-Comers, except R. L. Beeckman, and each runner-up except W. E. Glyn, are graduates or undergraduates of some college or university. Mr. Glyn is an Englishman and probably a graduate of some English university. The fact that almost all of these men were undergraduates, when they were first successful, would indicate that a college life affords the best training for this as well as the other sports.

CHAMPIONSHIP MATCH, NEWPORT CASINO, AUGUST 28, 1889.
(FROM A PHOTOGRAPH BY ALMAN.)

CHAPTER III.

THE CHAMPIONSHIPS OF THE U. S. N. L. T. A.

DOUBLES.

THE first championship of the United States in Doubles was decided at the Newport Casino in the year 1881, together with the Singles championship. Three distinct styles of playing the four-handed game were shown in this tournament. The majority of the players adopted the method which was then commonly employed in the single game; that is, both men stood at the base line and returned every ball from the bound. But the Philadelphia teams, notably Messrs. C. M. Clark and F. W. Taylor, and Messrs. Newbold and Van Rensselaer, had cultivated an entirely different style. By their system only one player remained in the back court, while the other was stationed close to the net, where he was always ready to pounce upon and "kill" any return which fell within his reach.

1st Round.	2d Round.	3d Round.	Final Round.
Gray and Shaw, 6-3, 6-1.			
Kessler and Glyn,	Gray and Shaw,		
Congdon and Gammell, 6-2, 6-3.	6-4, 6-3.	Gray and Shaw	
Morse and Caldwell,	Congdon and Gammell.		
Randolph and Rathbone, 6 5, 2-6, 6 3.		6-5. 6-4.	Newbold and Van Rensselaer
Hines and Cushman,	S. Powel and J. H. Powel.		
Newbold and Van Rensselaer, 6-5, 6-4.	Newbold and Van Rensselaer,	Newbold and Van Rensselaer.	
Rives and Stevens,			Champions: Clark and Taylor, 6-5, 6-4, 6-5.
Conover and Miller, 6-2, 6-2.	Conover and Miller.		
H. Powel and R. H. Powel,		Conover and Miller.	
Clark and Taylor, 6-5, 6-2.	Randolph and Rathbone.		
Nightingale and Smith		6-4, 6-3.	Clark and Taylor.
Dwight and Sears, 6-0, 6-0.	Dwight and Sears, 6-3, 6-1.		
Cogswell and Pruyn,		Clark and Taylor.	
S. Powel and J. H. Powel, a bye.	Clark and Taylor		

SCORE OF THE CHAMPIONSHIP TOURNAMENT OF 1881.

NEWPORT, AUGUST 31st.

(OLD SYSTEM OF DRAWING.)

1st Round.	2d Round.	3d Round.	Final Round.
C. M. Clark and F. W. Taylor, by default.	Dwight and Sears,		
Boit and Codman.		Dwight and Sears,	
Van Rensselaer and Newbold, 5-6, 6-2, 6-3.	6-5, 6-1.		
Rives and Stevens.	Powel and Johnson		Dwight and Sears.
Glyn and E. Thorne, 6-1, 5-6, 7-5.		6-5. 6-1.	
Rankine and Eldridge.	Van Rensselaer and Newbold,		
Nightingale and Smith, 6-0, 6-2.	6-3, 4-6, 9-7.	Clark and Taylor.	
Kneeland and Rathbone.	Conover and Miller.		Champions: Dwight and Sears. 6-2, 6-4, 6-4.
Conover and Miller, 6-3, 6-2.			
Congdon and Rhodes.	Nightingale and Smith,	Nightingale and Smith,	
Powel and Johnson 6-0, 6-2.	6-2, 1-6, 6-3.		
Denniston and Thomes	J. S. Clark and Dixon.		Nightingale and Smith.
J. S. Clark and Dixon. 3 6, 6 2, 6-1.		6-3. 6-2.	
Butler and Woodman.	C. M. Clark and Taylor,		
Dwight and Sears, a bye.	6-4, 6 0.	Van Rensselaer and Newbold.	
	Glyn and Thorne.		

SCORE OF THE CHAMPIONSHIP TOURNAMENT OF 1882,

NEWPORT, AUGUST 30th.

The third method was tried only by Messrs. Dwight and Sears, and by them with disastrous results. Both had improved their play in Singles by the adoption of the volleying game at the service line, and both accordingly thought that the same tactics would serve them well in the four-handed game. Their positions in the court did not differ from those assumed by players in the double game of to-day, with the single exception that the latter approach closer to the net.

The service line game of Messrs. Dwight and Sears was bound to be successful against the old fashioned base line play, and it won them an easy victory in their first match. It was decidedly different, however, when the succeeding round brought them against the more advanced methods of the Philadelphians, Clark and Taylor. The volleying of Dwight and Sears was so weak, being nothing more than tapping the ball, that the Philadelphian at the net was able to reach and "kill" almost all of their returns. Clark and Taylor, therefore, won an easy victory, and, in fact, no team was able to make any showing against them, except their fellow townsmen, Newbold and Van Rensselaer, who played the same style of game.

1882.

In August of this year the Doubles were again played at Newport, together with the Singles. The old-fashioned style of play had now almost entirely disappeared. The majority of the contesting teams, fifteen in all, adopted the Philadelphia game, while a few imitated Dwight and Sears. The Boston men now volleyed with much more severity and accuracy, and their double game was therefore much improved. They met Clark and Taylor, their rivals of the previous year, in the third round, and obtained revenge by defeating them in two straight sets. Messrs. Nightingale and Smith, of Providence, had now come to be the most skillful exponents of the Philadelphia style, but after defeating Newbold and Van Rensselaer in the third round, they were quite easily beaten in the final by Dwight and Sears, who thereby became the Doubles champions of the year.

1883.

During the early part of this year the champions of 1881, Messrs. C. M. Clark and F. W. Taylor, dissolved partnership, and Mr. J. S. Clark joined forces with his brother. The two brothers continued to play the same style of game, in which practice had made them almost perfect. They succeeded in defeating Messrs. Dwight and Sears at Boston, and repeated the victory in even more easy fashion in a return match, which was played on the grounds of the St. George's Cricket Club of New York. This last match was decided only just prior to the departure of the Messrs. Clark for England, where they afterwards met the Renshaw brothers. The victory at New York established their right to be considered the best exponents of the double game in the United States.

These two defeats were also instrumental in disorganizing the team work of Messrs. Dwight and Sears. They had previously begun to doubt the good policy of their service line game, and in the second match with the Clarks had relinquished it entirely, and adopted the system of their adver-

saries. This doubt and vacillation produced a curious effect upon their play in the next championship tournament. which was decided at Newport in the month of August. Instead of there clinging to their service-line game, or throwing it over in favor of the Clark style, Dwight and Sears adopted a mixture of the two. One played at the net, while the other remained at the service line. The adoption of such a policy would have been suicidal if the Clark brothers had been able to play in the tournament. But fortunately for the Bostonians, they were still abroad, and Dwight and Sears were individually so far superior to the remainder of the players, that they easily retained the championship, notwithstanding the defects in their system. Barring Dwight and Sears, Newbold and Van Rensselaer made the strongest pair.

1884.

Some months after the championship tournament of 1883, Dr. Dwight went abroad, and was afterwards joined by Mr. Sears. The experience of the two players in England, where they met the most skillful experts of that country, re-convinced them that the service-line game was the most effective. Having returned to this country in time for the next tournament, which was played at Newport in August, 1884, they found that they were not the only players who had become convinced of the strength of the service-line game. The best of the entries, including the Clark brothers, Knapp and Thorne, of Yale, and Van Rensselaer and Berry, had adopted this style of play. It had become a misnomer, however, to call it the *service-line game*, for the players did not ac-

1st Round.	2d Round.	3d Round.	Final Round.
F. Keene and J. S. Tooker, M. Paton and C. Munn. S. Powel and M. Fielding, 3-6, 6-5, 6-1. F. J. Brown and W. Merriman.	Newbold and Van Rensselaer, 6-1, 6-0. Conover and Brinley.	Newbold and Van Rensselaer.	Newbold and Van Rensselaer
A. Newbold and A. Van Rensselaer. 6-5, 6-4. Rathbone and H. A. Taylor. R. F. Conover and G. M. Brinley. 6-2, 6-1.		3-6, 6-5, 6-4.	Champions Dwight and Sears. 6-0, 6-2, 6-2.
G.M.Smith and W.Gammell,Jr Shaw and H. Leeds, 5 6, 6-0, 6-4. Johnson and H. W. H. Powel.	Shaw and Leeds, 6-2, 6-0. Powel and Fielding.	Shaw and Leeds.	
J. Dwight and R. D. Sears, 6-5, 6-0. C. Farnum and W. Dixon.	Dwight and Sears, 6-2, 6-0. Keene and Tooker.	Dwight and Sears, a bye.	Dwight and Sears,

SCORE OF THE CHAMPIONSHIP TOURNAMENT OF 1883.
NEWPORT, AUGUST 21st to 24th.

Preliminary Round.	1st Round.	2d Round.	3d Round.	Final Round.
C. M. Clark and J. S. Clark, 6-3, 6-1. Shaw and Powell. G. Richards and H. W. Slocum, Jr. 6-1, 6-0. F. W. Taylor and W. Lewis.	Clark and Clark, 6-2, 6-3. F. Brown and W. Merriman. W. V. S. Thorne and W. P. Knapp, 6-3, 6-2. P. Willis and P. Lyman.	Clark and Clark, 3-6, 6-2, 6-2. Thorne and Knapp.	Clark and Clark.	Dwight and Sears.
	J. Dwight and R. D. Sears, 6-0, 6-2. S. H. Hooper and F. K. Gillett. R. F. Conover and C. W. Barnes, by default. M. Paton and Partner.	Dwight and Sears, 6-0, 6-2. Conover and Barnes.	6 1, 1-6, 6-1. Dwight and Sears.	Champions Dwight and Sears. 6-4, 6-1, 8-10 6-4.
	A. Van Rensselaer and W. V. R. Berry, 6-4, 6-1. E. Butler and H. A. Taylor. F. Keene and J. S. Tooker, 4-6, 6-5, 6-2. R. L. Beeckman and M. Post.	Van Rensselaer and Berry. 6-1, 6-2. Keene and Tooker.	Van Rensselaer and Berry	Van Rensselaer and Berry.
	M. Fielding and E. Denniston, by default F. J. Hines and Partner G. M. Brinley and A. L. Stevens, 6-3, 3 6, 6 4. Richards and Slocum.	Fielding and Denniston, 6-4, 6-3. Brinley and Stevens.	6-1, 6-2. Brinley and Stevens.	

SCORE OF THE CHAMPIONSHIP TOURNAMENT OF 1884.
NEWPORT, AUGUST 20th to 23th.
(DRAWING BY BAGNALL-WILD SYSTEM.)

tually stand at the service line, but approached closer to the net.

Dwight and Sears effectually settled the question of superiority between themselves and the Clarks, for the year 1884, by defeating the Philadelphians in the third round. Van Rensselaer and Berry played a hard volleying game, and made a stubborn fight in the final round, but they, too, were finally obliged to succumb to Dwight and Sears, now champions for a third time.

1885.

As Dr. Dwight remained abroad during the entire summer of 1885, Mr. Sears was now obliged to defend his championship with another partner. Mr. C. M. Clark was prevented from playing by illness, and Mr. J. S. Clark therefore joined forces with Mr. Sears. This new combination was so strong that there was little doubt as to who would win the championship. Its most formidable rivals for the honor were Beeckman and H. A. Taylor, Moffatt and Davis, and Knapp and Slocum, all new teams. The last named player had joined Mr. Knapp in the absence of W. V. S. Thorne, his former partner. Knapp and Slocum succeeded in defeating both Moffatt and Davis and Beeckman and Taylor, and thus gained a place in the final round, where they were badly beaten by Sears and Clark.

1886.

The year 1886 witnessed another shifting about of partners. Such continual changes in the make-up of the prominent teams did much to injure the play in the four-handed game. The name of almost every player, who had been prominent in

Preliminary Round.	1st Round.	2d Round.	Final Round.
W. P. Knapp and H. W. Slocum, Jr. 6-2, 6-0. and F. W. Taylor and W. Lewis.	Knapp and Slocum, 6-3, 3-6, 6-4. Taylor and Beeckman.	Knapp and Slocum, 8-6, 7-5.	Knapp and Slocum.
M. Fielding and Corse, by default. M. Paton and Partner. A. Moffat and C. B. Davis, 6-3, 6-2. H. Morgan and Miller.	Fielding and Corse 6-3, 4-6, 6-3. Moffat and Davis.	Moffat and Davis.	Champions, Sears and Clark 6-3, 6-0, 6-2.
H. A. Taylor and R. L. Beeckman, 7-5, 6-4. S. H. Hooper and F. S. Mansfield.	R. D. Sears and J. S. Clark, 6-2, 6-3. Smith and Nightingale.	Sears and Clark.	Sears and Clark.
P. E. Presbrey and F. H. Gillett, 6-4, 3-6, 6-2. W. V. R. Berry and A. Van Rensselaer.	Presbrey and Gillett, 6-3, 6-2. Stokes and Howe.	6-4, 6-2. Presbrey and Gillett.	

SCORE OF THE CHAMPIONSHIP TOURNAMENT OF 1885,
NEWPORT, AUGUST 18TH TO 21ST.

Preliminary Round.	1st Round.	2d Round.	Final Round.
F. S. Mansfield and S. H. Hooper, 6-2, 6-3, 3-6, 4-6, 6-3. W. H. Barnes and O. S. Campbell.	J. Dwight and R. D. Sears, 6 2, 6-1, 6-0. Mansfield and Hooper.	Dwight and Sears,	Dwight and Sears.
F. W. Taylor and W. Lewis, 6-4, 6-5, 6-1. —. Gamble and G. McKenzie. J. S. Clark and W. V. R. Berry, 6-4, 6-2, 4-6, 0-6, 8 6. C. A. Chase and Q. A. Shaw, Jr.	Taylor and Lewis, by default. Clark and Berry.	6-5, 6-4, 3-6, 6-3. Clark and Berry.	Dwight and Sears.
M. Fielding and d'Invilliers, 5-6, 6-5, 3-6, 6-4. Tucker and A.L.Rives. R. L. Beeckman and H. W. Slocum, Jr. 6-0, 6-1, 6-5.	Beeckman and Slocum, by default. Fielding and d'Invilliers.	Beeckman and Slocum,	Champions, Dwight and Sears. 7-5, 5-7, 7-5, 6-4.
Nightingale and Smith. P. S. Sears and H. M. Sears, by default. Robbins and Robbins.	H. A. Taylor and G. M. Brinley, 6-1, 6-4, 6-4. P. S. Sears and H. M. Sears.	6-3,6-2,0-6,1-6, 10-8. Taylor and Brinley.	Taylor and Brinley.

SCORE OF THE CHAMPIONSHIP TOURNAMENT OF 1886.
NEWPORT, AUGUST 23D TO 28TH.

the Doubles of 1885, again appeared in the entry list of the Newport tournament of 1886, but the combination of names was different in every case. Dr. Dwight returned from England, and once more entered with Mr. Sears. H. A. Taylor played with Brinley; Slocum with Beeckman, and J. S. Clark with W. V. R. Berry. P. S. and H. M. Sears, twin brothers of the champion, now appeared for the first time and made an interesting pair, but were easily defeated in one of the early rounds by Taylor and Brinley. The latter team made a record which was alike surprising and remarkable. They defeated Beeckman and Slocum in a hard match of five sets, and were within an ace of conquering the champions in the final round. This final contest was the most beautiful exhibition of the double game ever seen at Newport. Taylor and Brinley not only won the first set, but also made the score of the second 5–4 and 40-0 in their favor. If they could have scored but one more point at that time, it is not only possible, but decidedly probable that the championship of 1886 would have been theirs. As it happens quite often, however, the one last point was the hardest of all to win. Dwight and Sears made a successful stand, won the set and finally the next two. The play throughout was marked by long and beautiful rallies, and the victory was secured mainly by the superior position play of the champions, who stood close to the net and continually forced their adversaries to the back of the court. Both members of the defeated team were left-handed, and both played with all the dash and grace which seems peculiar to left-handed players.

1887.

A very important step was taken at the annual convention of the National Association, which was held in the month of March. The resolution, requiring that all matches in the championship tournaments should be the best three out of five sets, had been passed and carried into effect the previous year, and it had then been discovered that the playing of such long matches, both in Singles and Doubles, produced too great a strain upon the endurance of the average contestant. It was now determined, therefore, that while the Singles championship should still be decided at Newport, the Doubles must be played elsewhere, and at a different season of the year. The grounds of the Orange Lawn Tennis Club, at Mountain Station, N. J., were selected as the best for the purpose, and the second week in September was fixed as the time. This was about ten days after the championship in Singles had been decided.

The tournament was a failure for several reasons. The majority of the players become tired of Lawn Tennis after the Newport tournament is decided, and usually lay aside their rackets for the season. There were therefore only twelve entries in all, and of these the veteran players appeared in unusually bad form. Continuous rainy weather put an additional damper upon the sport.

The most interesting feature was the entry of Messrs. McClellan and Cummins, the champion team of the West. They had the bad fortune to be drawn against Messrs. Dwight and Sears in the preliminary round, but the latter pair were in such poor form, that during the early part of the match

PHOTO ERIC SADLY

Valentine Estall

it seemed as if the Western champions would con-
quer those of the East. Dwight and Sears improved, however, and secured the victory after five
sets had been played. They then had an almost
similar experience against Post and Coffin in the
first round.

Another pair of veterans, J. S. Clark and G. M.
Brinley, also failed to do themselves justice, and
were defeated by O. S. Campbell and A. Duryee,
two of the youngest players in the competition.
The latter in turn were obliged to succumb to
another veteran team, H. A. Taylor and Slocum.
Dwight and Sears met Taylor and Slocum in the
final round, and here again it became necessary to
play the full five sets before the former won the
match, and with it the championship of the United
States for the fifth time.

1888.

At the next meeting of the Association, it was
decided by an extremely close vote to hold the
Doubles tournament of 1888 at Staten Island, instead of Orange. The grounds of the Staten Island
Cricket and Base Ball Club were in every way
suitable for the purpose, but the moving causes of
the previous year were again instrumental in pre-
venting the tournament from being a complete
success.

The dates selected, September 12th, 13th, and
14th, were, as before, altogether too late in the
season. Only ten teams entered, and most of these
were from the neighborhood of New York. Messrs.
McClellan and Cummins, however, once more came
from the West to try conclusions with Eastern
players. Mr. R. D. Sears' injury had obliged him

Preliminary Round.	1st Round.	2d Round.	Final Round
S. M. Colgate and Partner, F. M. Carryl and Partner.	Colgate and W. A. Brown, 7-5, 6-2, 6-0. Carryl and Watson.	Colgate and Brown,	
C. J. Post and S. V. Coffin 6-4, 6-3, 6 1. M. S. Paton and Partner. R. D. Sears and J. Dwight. 4-6, 6 3, 2-6, 6-1, 6-1.	Post and Coffin, 4-6, 11-9, 6-2, 6-4. Sears and Dwight.	6-1, 6-1, 7-5. Sears and Dwight.	Sears and Dwight.
B. F. Cummins and E. B. McClellan. O. S. Campbell and A. Duryee, 6 2, 2-6, 6-1, 3-6 6-2.	Campbell and Duryee.		Champions: Sears and Dwight. 6-4, 3-6, 2-6, 6-3, 6-3.
J. S. Clark and G. M. Brinley H. A. Taylor and H. W. Slocum, Jr. 6 2, 6-3, 6-1.	6-2, 10-8, 4-6, 6-3. Taylor and Slocum.	Taylor and Slocum.	
S. Campbell, Jr. and B. J. Carroll. A. E. Wright and M. R. Wright, by default.	Wright and Wright	6-3, 6-4, 1-6, 6-2.	Taylor and Slocum.
C. F. Watson and Partner. Q. A. Shaw, Jr. and T. S. Tailer.	6-1, 6-2, 4-6, 6-2. Shaw and Tailer.	Shaw and Tailer.	

SCORE OF THE CHAMPIONSHIP TOURNAMENT OF 1887,

MOUNTAIN STATION, N. J., SEPT. 6TH TO 9TH.

Preliminary Round.	1st Round.	2d Round.	Final Round.
M. S. Paton and C. E. Sands, 3-6, 1-6, 6-1, 7-5, 9-7. A. Torrence and M. H. Torrence.	Torrence and Torrence, 6 3, 6-4, 6-3. H. A. Taylor and J. S. Clark.	Taylor and Clark,	
E. P. McMullen and C. Hobart, 6-3, 7 5, 6 0. W. E. Glyn and M. F. Goodbody.	V. G. Hall and O. S. Campbell, 6-2, 6 1, 6-1. C. J. Post and W. A. Tomes.	6-2, 3-6, 7-5, 6 3 Hall and Campbell.	Hall and Campbell.
J. Dwight and Q. A. Shaw, Jr. by default. R. V. Beach and C. H. Ludington.	B. F. Cummins and E. B. McClellan, 6-3, 4-6, 6-4, 7-9, 6-4. Beach and Ludington.	Cummins and McClellan.	Champions: Hall and Campbell. 6 4, 6-2, 6-4.
	H. W. Slocum, Jr. and F. Keene. 6-2, 3-6, 4-6, 7-5, 6-3. McMullen and Hobart.	6-2, 5-7, 6-4, 6 3 McMullen and Hobart	McMullen and Hobart.

SCORE OF THE CHAMPIONSHIP TOURNAMENT OF 1888,

STATEN ISLAND, SEPT. 12TH TO 16TH.

to withdraw altogether, and his former partner,
Dr. Dwight, was also absent. This was therefore
the first tournament of the Association, since its
organization in 1881, in which neither of these
sterling players appeared as a competitor. In addition, a succession of rainy days had softened the
courts and rendered them almost unfit for play.

But notwithstanding all this, some of the playing was decidedly good. The chief honors went to
a new combination, consisting of Messrs. O. S.
Campbell and V. G. Hall, who lost but a single set
in the entire play, and that to Messrs. H. A. Taylor and J. S. Clark. Mr. Foxhall Keene and Mr.
H. W. Slocum, Jr. had formed a partnership, but
they were defeated in the first round by another
New York team, Messrs. McMullen and Hobart.
The latter seemed unable to stand against the
magnificent net play of Hall and Campbell, and
were easily beaten by them in the final round.
Hall and Campbell, at the time of winning this
championship, were still undergraduates of Columbia College. To them belongs the honor of
bringing the Doubles championship to New York
for the first time.

1889.

The experience of the last two years had now
taught its lesson, and the Association determined
to play the Doubles during the first week in July,
hoping that the early-summer enthusiasm of the
players would swell the entry list to greater pro-
portions. The well kept grounds of the Staten
Island Club were again selected, but the tournament was hardly a success. The number of entries
was even smaller than before, and a storm of unusual

violence caused a postponement for an entire week. The playing would call for but little comment had it not been for its brilliant termination. Messrs. H. A. Taylor and H. W. Slocum, Jr., met Messrs. O. S. Campbell and V. G. Hall, the champions of 1888, in the final round, and this match, played in the presence of a large and enthusiastic crowd of spectators, was remarkable in many respects. While the rallies were long and brilliant, the volleying was nevertheless accurate and hard. Every set was close and fought to the bitter end. Forty-four games were played before the first two sets were decided. Taken all in all, it was perhaps the most interesting match in the history of the Doubles championships, with the possible exception of that played by Dwight and Sears

Preliminary Round.	1st Round.	2d Round.	Final Round.
A. E. Wright and D. Miller, 6-4, 7-5, 6-2. L. W. Glazebrook and F. L. V. Hoppin.	Wright and Miller, 6-4, 6-3, 6-4. F. G. Beach and R. P. Huntington, Jr.	Beach and Huntington, 6-3, 6-3, 6-1.	Taylor and Slocum,
C. Hobart and A. W. Post, 6-2, 6-2, 8-6. C. J. Post, Jr. and S. V. Coffin.	Hobart and Post, 8-6, 6-4, 6-2. H. A. Taylor and H. W. Slocum, Jr.	Taylor and Slocum.	Champions: Taylor and Slocum. 14-12, 10-8, 6-4.
	J. A. Rome and G. A. Willis, 6-1, 4-6, 8-6, 6-1. S. W. Smith and M. DeGarmendia.	Rome and Willis, 9-7, 3-6, 6-1, 6-3.	Hall and Campbell.
	V. G. Hall and O. S. Campbell, 6-3, 6-3, 6-1. F. D. Pavey and W. A. Tomes.	Hall and Campbell	

SCORE OF THE CHAMPIONSHIP TOURNAMENT OF 1889.

STATEN ISLAND, JULY 1st to 10th.

against Brinley and Taylor in the Newport tournament of 1886. Taylor and Slocum finally won, however, in three straight sets, thus completing the tournament and securing the championship for 1889, without losing a single set.

The following table gives in condensed form the main facts relating to the Doubles championships, from 1881 to 1889, inclusive:

DOUBLES CHAMPIONSHIPS.

YEAR	PLAYED AT	CHAMPIONS.	RUNNERS-UP.
1881	Newport.	C. M. Clark and F.W.Taylor.	A. Newbold, A.Van Rensselaer.
1882	Newport.	R. D. Sears and J. Dwight.	G. A. Smith, Nightingale.
1883	Newport.	R. D. Sears and J. Dwight.	A. Newbold. A. Van Rensselaer.
1884	Newport.	R. D. Sears and J. Dwight.	W. V. R. Berry, A. VanRensselaer.
1885	Newport.	R. D. Sears and J. S. Clark.	W. P. Knapp, II.W. Slocum, Jr.
1886	Newport.	R. D. Sears and J. Dwight.	H. A. Taylor, G. M. Brinley.
1887	Orange,N.J.	R. D. Sears and J. Dwight.	H. A. Taylor, H. W. Slocum, Jr.
1888	Staten Isl'd.	V.G.Hall and O.S. Campbell.	E. P. McMullen, C. Hobart.
1889	Staten Isl'd.	H. A. Taylor and H. W. Slocum, Jr.	V. G. Hall, O. S. Campbell.

CHAPTER IV.

OUR PLAYERS ABROAD.

MESSRS. C. M. and J. S. Clark, of Philadelphia, were the first of our representative players to journey abroad and try conclusions with the champions of England. In the early summer of 1883, the Clark brothers were close rivals of Messrs. Dwight and Sears for the honor of being considered the best exponents of the double game in the United States. These two teams were far superior to all others. To settle the question of supremacy between themselves, two matches were played, one at Boston on the 21st of June, and another at New York five days later, both of which were won by the Clarks. Having thus fairly earned the foremost place among our double players, the Philadelphians sailed for England, and immediately upon their arrival, arranged a four-handed match with the Renshaw brothers, the famous champions. It must not be understood that the Clarks went abroad with the sole idea of

Joseph S Clark.

representing the United States in an international contest. Having secured the foremost place in their own country, it was but natural, as an incident of their foreign trip, that they should desire to meet the more experienced players of England.

The first match with the Renshaws was played on the All England Club ground at Wimbledon, on the 18th of July, 1883. The Clarks played one man at the net and the other in the back court, and made a very creditable showing against the volleying game of the English champions. They lost the first set, and also the second, but the latter only after they had been within one point of winning it. The third they won easily. The final score in favor of the Renshaws was 6–4, 8–6, 3–6, 6–1.

The American players were not entirely satisfied with the result of this contest, and a return match was therefore played. The following report is taken from the "London Field:"

"The return match was played off on Monday, July 23d, on the All England Club ground at Wimbledon, and once more resulted in a victory for the home team even still more easily than on the previous occasion, the Cheltenham pair now gaining three sets in succession, and eighteen games to eight. Seven games out of the eighteen were called deuce; in one of them—the opening game of the second set—advantage and deuce was called eight times, and two were love games to the English pair and one to the Americans. The Messrs. Renshaw played better together than in the first match, but still did not show up in the form that they have been seen to play in. Their fault now seems to be that they are too much at the net together. This, of course, at times, when they have their opponents at a disadvantage, is no doubt a winning game, but when done as a rule, too often causes them to play on the defensive, when if they had bided their time, they would have themselves been able to assume the offensive. The Americans are certainly good servers, being far more sure of their first services than a majority of English players. Their service might be called the round-arm over-hand, as it is really a mixture of the two. As a rule, their net man stands too close to the net, though at times he makes some beautiful short strokes, but the English pair found that it was not a difficult task to return the ball down the side lines out of his reach."

The Clarks also played with varying fortune in both the Singles and Doubles of several English tournaments. They captured a number of prizes, but perhaps their most notable performance was in the Redhills tournament, near London. Here Mr. J. S. Clark took second prize in Singles, and the two brothers won their way into the final round of Doubles, where they met Messrs. Lewis and Williams, two excellent players. The Americans had won two sets out of the first three, when rain interfered with the completion of the match, and the Clarks foolishly agreed to finish at the conclusion of their second contest with the Renshaws. The agreement was carried out, however, and Lewis and Williams won the two remaining sets and the first prizes in Doubles.

Late in the autumn of 1883, Dr. James Dwight, of Boston, journeyed to England with the intention of meeting the Lawn Tennis "cracks" of that country. He bore letters of introduction to Mr. Wm. Renshaw, and almost immediately upon his arrival was able to secure an afternoon's play with the English champion in the Maida Vale covered court. Soon afterwards Dr. Dwight departed for Cannes, in the south of France, and there spent the winter in company with Messrs.W. Renshaw, Farrer, and Grove, all English players of prominence. Mr. R. D. Sears, Dr. Dwight's partner in Doubles, also joined the party early in the spring. The winter practice of these players upon the gravel courts at Cannes, the most perfect in the world, enabled them to open the season of 1884 in the best of form.

The first notable tournament of 1884, in which the Americans competed, was the Irish championship meeting, held at Fitzwilliam Square, in the city of Dublin. In addition to Messrs. Dwight and Sears, Mr. A. L. Rives, also of Boston, was among the entries. Mr. B. S. De Garmendia, too, although accredited to France, was really a representative of the United States, where he has since been prominent in various departments of athletics, but particularly during recent years as the champion of the New York Racket Court Club. Mr. De Garmendia and Mr. Rives were defeated in their first matches, but Dr. Dwight and Mr. Sears made a very creditable showing. Dr. Dwight won a place in the third round, where he was defeated by H. M. McKay, one of the strongest players among the Englishmen—(6–3, 6–4, 6–3). Mr. Sears performed still better. He played through the first three rounds without losing a set, and in the fourth made a strong stand, especially in the first set, against the famous H. F. Lawford, who afterwards won the tournament and defeated E. Renshaw for the championship of Ireland. The score of Lawford against Sears was 6–4, 6–3, 6–2, and that of Lawford vs. E. Renshaw was 6–1, 6–4, 6–2. Although no one would think of claiming that Mr. Sears was the equal of Mr. E. Renshaw at this time, it was nevertheless creditable, that of the two players, the American should have succeeded in winning the greater number of games from Lawford.

In the doubles, Messrs. Dwight and Sears were unfortunate enough to draw against E. L. Williams and E. Lewis, one of the strongest teams, in the first round. They were defeated, 7–5, 6–0.

Directly after the Irish championship meeting, Messrs. Dwight and Sears were entered at the Bath tournament, but Mr. Sears injured his foot and was obliged to withdraw, while Dr. Dwight was defeated in the first round of Singles. At Cheltenham Mr. Sears won a place in the final round, and was then defeated by a strong player, Mr. Donald Stewart—(10–8, 6–1, 6–3). Dwight and Sears should have won the Doubles at the same place, but after being within one point of winning the final match, they went entirely to pieces, and were defeated by Capt. C. K. Wood and C. L. Sweet— (6–3, 3–6, 2–6, 6–5, 6–0).

At the Northern tournament, held in the vicinity of Liverpool, the Americans made a still better record. It is a singular coincidence, that in the second round of the Singles, Messrs. Dwight and Sears should have drawn against and defeated Mr. J. B. Ismay and Mr. J. A. Rome, both Englishmen, who have since become residents of the United States. Dwight and Sears were then successively defeated by Donald Stewart, who won the tournament. In the Doubles Messrs. Dwight and Sears were entirely successful, beating H. W. Wilberforce and H. V. Macnachten in the final round—

(2-6, 6-1, 6-4, 8-6). This victory brought them against the Renshaw brothers for the northern championship, and thus the Doubles Champions of England and the United States were for the first time matched in tournament play. The Renshaws of course won, but the three sets were well played and exciting—(6-2, 6-4, 6-3).

The All England championships were held at Wimbledon in July, and here again Mr. Sears was unable to compete in the Singles, this time on account of an injured wrist. Dr. Dwight played, however, and easily won his first match. In the second round he was defeated by H. Chipp, but not until five hard sets had been played. It would appear from the following account (from "London Pastime") of the final and deciding set, that ill luck had much to do with the Doctor's defeat:

"The score standing at two sets all, ends were changed with every game. Dwight secured the first game to thirty, and Chipp brought matters even by winning the next at the same score. Dwight won the next four games, two being love ones and one at deuce, thus making the score 5-1 in his favor. Chipp woke up a little and won the next game to fifteen, but the eighth was very hotly contested, deuce being called six times, and Dwight being three times within one point of winning the match. A false bound had now a great effect upon the game, the American being the sufferer, and Chipp won. He also secured the next two games to thirty, and 'games all' was called. Chipp still having some good luck, next won a love game, and winning the twelfth to thirty, secured the set and match after one of the best contests of the meeting. The battle of the styles was fought again in this match, Dwight being a volleyer of the most pronounced type, while Chipp relies solely on his back play. Dwight's volleying and general play was very much admired, and though beaten, he was far, very far from being disgraced."

The Singles were won by H. F. Lawford, who was then defeated by W. Renshaw for the championship—(6-0, 6-4, 9-7).

In the first round of Doubles, Dwight and Sears defeated J. T. Hartley and R. T. Richardson (6-2, 6-3, 8-6), a team which had won the championship of England in 1882. In the second round they drew a bye, but in the third met their Waterloo at the hands of W. and E. Renshaw (6-0, 6-1, 6-2,) who then defeated E. Lewis and E. L. Williams, and thereby won the Doubles championship for 1884.

Immediately after the championships were decided, Messrs. Sears and Dwight returned to the United States, the former bringing with him the racket with which W. Renshaw had won the English championships of 1882 and 1883.

Shortly after the season of play in the United States had ended, Dr. Dwight again went abroad, and, as before, spent the entire winter at Cannes, in the company of W. Renshaw, H. Grove, G. H. Taylor, and other English players of note. The beginning of 1885 found Dr. Dwight in much better form than at any time during the previous year, and his record of the entire season was so brilliant as to earn for him a high place among the English experts. He opened the season by winning both Singles and Doubles at Brighton, the latter event with C. H. A. Ross as a partner. After this victory he was a competitor in all the notable English tournaments, and almost always succeeded in carrying off a first prize, either in Singles or Doubles. His usual partner in Doubles was E. Lewis, but he also played in different tournaments with W. Renshaw, Donald Stewart, H. Grove and J. C. McKay.

Dr. Dwight's most notable performance of the year, however, was in the Northern Championship meeting at Manchester. There he not only succeeded in winning the tournament, defeating E. Lewis in the final round (8–6, 6–0, 6–4), but also followed this by wresting the Northern Championship from Donald Stewart, the holder—(6–2, 6–4, 6–4). In the Doubles, Dwight and Lewis gained a place in the final round, but were there defeated by the Renshaw brothers—(6–1, 6–1, 7–5).

In the All England Championships, also, Dr. Dwight made a creditable record. He was possibly nerved to greater effort by the fact that this tournament was begun on the Fourth of July. He played through the first three rounds without losing a set, and finally succumbed (6–2, 6–2, 6–3) only to the great Lawford, who was then at his best. That Dwight's defeat was not a discreditable one is shown by the fact that in the following round Lawford also defeated E. Renshaw, and afterwards made a most stubborn fight against W. Renshaw for the championship—(7–5, 6–2, 4–6, 7–5).

In the championship Doubles, Dwight and Lewis defeated such a strong team as Chipp and E. Barratt-Smith (6–3, 6–0, 11–9), and made a magnificent struggle against the champion Renshaws, winning one set and losing two others by close scores. The final score in favor of the Renshaws was 4–6, 6–1, 6–4, 6–4.

During the entire season of 1885, Dr. Dwight took part in thirteen tournaments. In almost all of these he played in both Singles and Doubles, and frequently in the Ladies and Gentlemen's Doubles. He won in all thirteen first and eight second prizes.

At the end of each year's play, it has been the custom of "London Pastime" to publish a classification of the prominent players, based upon the records of the entire season. The following, which was published in 1885, shows Dr. Dwight's position among the English experts of that year :

W. Renshaw	Scratch
H. F. Lawford	2 Bisques
E. Renshaw	Half 15
E. de S. H. Browne . } E. Chatterton . . . . . }	Half 15 and 1 Bisque
W. J. Hamilton	Half 15 and 2 Bisques
H. K. McKay	15
Hon. P. B. Lyon . . . . ⎫ H. Chipp . . . . . ⎬ J. Dwight . . . . ⎪ E. Lewis . . . . ⎭	15 and 1 Bisque
H. Grove . . . . } C. H. A. Ross . . . . . . }	15 and 2 Bisques
W. C. Taylor	Half 30

Dr. Dwight returned to the United States too late to compete in the Newport tournament of 1885. The following winter, like the two previous, was spent at Cannes. Messrs. E. Renshaw, Grove, Stanley, and R. D. Sears were also there. The latter, however, was obliged to return to the United States before the close of the winter. Early in the spring of 1886, Mr. R. L. Beeckman, of New York, joined the colony of players. Shortly after his arrival, a handicap tournament

was arranged, and proved to be very interesting.
Mr. E. Renshaw was placed in a class by himself,
owing half fifteen, and in addition conceding 1
bisque to the players of Class II., who were Messrs.
Dwight, Grove and Beeckman. The remaining
contestants received large handicaps. Curiously
enough, Mr. Renshaw won the prize by successively defeating each player of Class II. He
won from Dr. Dwight in three straight sets;
from Mr. Grove by three sets to one, and from Mr.
Beeckman, in the final round, by three sets to two.
The latter played in admirable form, and was defeated only by the following close score—6-4, 5-7,
6-3, 4-6, 6-4.

During the playing season of 1886, Mr. Dwight
once more participated in the English tournaments,
but not so frequently as in 1885, nor with such
brilliant success. His most notable victory was
won at the Bath meeting, where he defeated the
famous Irish player, E. de S. H. Browne, and also
H. Grove, thereby winning the West of England
Championship. He was beaten by Browne at
Cheltenham, however, and a week later, at Liverpool, was compelled to relinquish the Northern
championship to Grove. This last defeat was certainly not a discreditable one, for Grove was playing in magnificent form, and had already won from
E. Renshaw before meeting Dr. Dwight. Dwight
and Grove played together in the Doubles, and
won the All-Comers tournament, but were defeated
by W. and E. Renshaw for the Northern Championship.

This virtually completed Dr. Dwight's foreign
play for the season of 1886. Without remaining

for the decision of the All-England Championships, he returned to the United States, and afterwards played in the All-Comers tournament at Newport. (Part II. Chap. II.) Later in the year the "London Pastime" published a short sketch of Dr. Dwight's career, from which the following is an extract:

"The strength of Dwight's game consists in his wonderful proficiency in volleying, in which he is equalled by one or two players, at most; its weakness is his back-play, although he has lately made some improvement in this respect. He is especially good at volleying tosses and high-pitched balls, which he returns with great certainty and considerable force. What is, however, especially worthy of notice, is his wonderful knowledge of the game, the excellent judgment with which he takes note of the weak points of his antagonist, and the manner in which he avails himself of any openings that present themselves in the heat of contest. He has an unequalled mastery of the theory of the modern game, which he has ably formulated after careful study of the examples of the English champion and other great players, with whom he has for some three years had the advantage of almost daily practice."

At the end of the year 1886, "Pastime" also published the following classification, showing that Dr. Dwight had more than held his own since the classification of 1885:

W. Renshaw	Scratch
H. F. Lawford	2 Bisques
E. L. Lewis	⎫
H. Grove	⎪
E. Renshaw	⎬ Half 15
E. de S. H. Browne	⎪
Eyre, Chatterton	⎭
W. J. Hamilton	⎫
J. Dwight	⎬ Half 15 and 1 Bisque
F. L. Williams	⎭

H. W. W. Wilberforce . Half 15 and 2 Bisques
P. B. Lyon . . . . ⎫
H. Chipp . . . . ⎬ 15
C. L. Sweet . . . . ⎭
C. H. A. Ross . . . . . ⎫
W. N. Cobold . . . . . ⎬ 15 and one Bisque
J. H. Crispe . . . . ⎫
J. R. Deykin . . . . ⎬ 15 and 5 Bisques
E. G. Meers . . . . ⎭

Dr. Dwight also spent the summer of 1887 in
England but played in only a few of the tournaments. He lost the West of England championship to Grove, but captured the Singles at Leam-
ington, and elsewhere added to the laurels which
he had won during the three previous years. This
was his last experience in England, however, and
as no other representative player of the United
States has ventured abroad during recent years,
we have since had no test of the comparative
merits of the players of the two countries, except
such as was afforded by the visit of Mr. E. G. Meers
to the United States in the summer of 1889. (Part
II. Chap. II.)

CHAPTER V.

THE INTER-COLLEGIATE ASSOCIATION.

NO HISTORY of Lawn Tennis in the United States would be complete without some reference to the Inter-Collegiate Association. The tournaments of this Association have been second only to the national championships in importance and interest; and naturally so, for it is the college players, in almost every year, who have gained the highest distinction in Lawn Tennis.

The organization of the Inter-Collegiate Association was decidedly informal. Lawn Tennis had been so rapidly gaining a place in popular favor that finally, in the spring of 1883, the representative players of some of the larger colleges came to the conclusion that the game ought to be recognized in some degree as a college sport. Correspondence followed, and on the 5th of June, 1883, representatives of Harvard, Yale, Brown, Amherst and Trinity met

Philip S. Sears.

at Hartford, the seat of the last named college, and organized the Inter-Collegiate Lawn Tennis Association. Mr. J. S. Clark was chosen as the first president.

The Association was no sooner organized than it proceeded to hold its first championship meeting (June 6th and 7th). This tournament was played on the beautiful grounds of the Hartford Retreat for the Insane, and among the spectators were many of the insane patients, who appeared to thoroughly appreciate the efforts of the contestants. Harvard was represented by J. S. Clark in the Singles, and by the same player, with H. A. Taylor, in the Doubles; Yale, by G. L. Sargent in the Singles, and by H. W. Slocum, Jr. and W. C. Camp, the famous Foot-Ball player, in the Doubles; Brown, by Barker in the Singles, and Barker and Hill in the Doubles; while Amherst and Trinity were also represented in both events.

Mr. R. D. Sears was then a senior at Harvard, but was prevented by illness from competing in this tournament. It is not generally known that Mr. J. S. Clark was at this time nearly, if not quite, equal in skill to Mr. Sears. He had defeated him in the Harvard College tournament, and repeated the victory in a match which was contested at Longwood shortly after the Inter-Collegiate tournament had been decided. It is small wonder, then, that Mr. Clark should have proved an easy winner of the first inter-collegiate contest. He defeated Sargent of Yale, Barker of Brown, Curts of Trinity and Comstock of Amherst in rapid succession, and Sargent won second place for Yale by defeating all of the others, except Clark. Harvard also captured the

championship in Doubles, Clark and Taylor winning with ease from each team, except Hill and
Barker, of Brown, who made a hard fight for the
honor, and lost the final and deciding set only by
the close score of 7–5.

It was shortly afterwards decided that the autumn
was, for many reasons, a better season of the year
in which to hold an inter-collegiate contest in Lawn
Tennis, and another tournament was accordingly
played in October, 1883.   The grounds of the Hartford Retreat for the Insane were again selected, and
the same colleges were represented, but this time
by entirely different players.   Harvard and Yale
again furnished by far the best of the entries, and
the remainder of the colleges were hardly in the
fight.   H. A. Taylor won the championship in Singles for Harvard, his nearest opponents being W.
V. S Thorne and W. P. Knapp, of Yale.   The two
last named players made a strong fight in the
Doubles against H. A. Taylor and P. E. Presbrey,
but that championship, like all the others, finally
went to Harvard.

Up to this time, Harvard had enjoyed a monopoly
in the winning of championships, but a break in her
series of victories was soon to come.   The colleges
again met at Hartford in October, 1884, and several
new members of the Association, including Princeton and Wesleyan, now sent representatives. Trinity
was represented by Mr. G. M. Brinley, and for the
first time became an important factor in the struggle.
Mr. R. D. Sears had entered the Medical School of
Harvard University, and as he now appeared in company with Mr. H. A. Taylor, it seemed almost cer-

tain that Harvard would repeat her successes of the two previous years.

The tournament was a memorable one, marked as it was by one of the few defeats which Mr. Sears has sustained in this country. As the play in Singles progressed, the issue narrowed down to four men, Sears and Taylor of Harvard, Knapp of Yale, and Brinley of Trinity. Knapp was drawn against Sears, and, to the intense surprise of every one, defeated the champion of the United States with comparative ease. While great credit was due the Yale man, it is not unfair to say that the poor condition of the turf courts was largely responsible for Sears' defeat. Knapp played a typical volleying game, gaining his position at the net at all hazards, while Sears was altogether too content to remain in the back court, trusting to pass his adversary. A number of bad bounds did much to injure his chances, and Knapp was not slow in taking advantage of the circumstances.

The misfortunes of Harvard did not come singly, however. After Taylor had won the first set from Brinley and had made a good beginning in the second, he fell and sprained his wrist so badly as to necessitate his withdrawal. Thus Trinity and Yale were left to contest the final round, and although Brinley won the first two sets and lacked but a single game of the third, Knapp still persisted and was finally rewarded by securing Yale's first championship in Lawn Tennis.

Sears and Taylor having been obliged to withdraw also from the Doubles, that championship likewise went to Yale, Knapp and Thorne defeating Brinley and Paddock, of Trinity, in the final round.

The turf courts at Hartford had been so unsatisfactory throughout the last meeting, that the Association now decided, for this as well as other reasons,
to hold the next tournament on the grounds of the
New Haven Lawn Club, an organization located in
the same city, but having no connection whatever
with Yale College. Some of the players objected
to earth courts, which are universally used in New
Haven, but the situation of the club was so central
and the management of the first tournament so satisfactory, that the Association has never since seen
fit to make a change.

The championship tournament of 1885 was begun
on the 15th of October. The membership of the Association had now largely increased, Amherst, Brown,
Lehigh, Princeton, Trinity, Williams, Wesleyan and
Yale sending representatives. As many as twenty-
two players were entered, the most prominent of
whom were the Sears brothers of Harvard, Larkin
of Princeton, C. A. Chase of Amherst, Brinley and
Paddock of Trinity, Davis of Lehigh, and Knapp
and Thacher of Yale. Kabayama, a young Jap-
anese student of Wesleyan, was also among the
entries.

The Singles were chiefly notable for the unex-
pectedly good play of Mr. A. Duryee, a prominent
athlete of Williams College. He won his way into
the final round, and there met the Yale representative, Knapp, who had won the championship in 1884.
This match was long and well fought, Yale finally
winning by the following remarkable score, 10–8,
10–8, 6–3.

Mr. W. V. S. Thorne, Knapp's former partner,
had graduated from Yale, but the latter, with H. W.

Robert P. Huntington Jr.

Shipman, succeeded in retaining the championship
in Doubles for Yale, Brinley and Paddock, of Trinity, again making the hardest fight.

The championship meeting of 1886 was also very
successful. It was held in October on the grounds
of the New Haven Lawn Club. Columbia and
Cornell had recently joined the Association, but the
latter sent no representatives. Columbia's players
were Messrs. V. G. Hall, J. Bacon, C. E. Sands,
Smith and Strebeigh.

The tournament was remarkable for the brilliant
work of Brinley, of Trinity. Knapp of Yale, who
had been the only one to defeat the Trinity player
in 1884 and 1885, was now absent from the Singles,
and Brinley won the championship without losing a
single set. A fair sample of his excellent play was
shown in the final match against P. S. Sears of Harvard. Although the latter was an excellent player
and appeared in good form, Brinley scored the first
eleven games in rapid succession, allowing his adversary only an occasional point.

Mr. Knapp was in the Doubles, however, and this
time with still another partner, Mr. W. L. Thacher.
For the third year in succession, the Doubles Championship became an issue between Knapp and partner, of Yale, and Brinley and Paddock, of Trinity,
and once more did Knapp's presence prove disastrous
to Trinity's chances. Four sets were played, all
close and exciting, but the championship finally
went to Yale by the following score, 7–9, 7–5, 7–5,
6–4.

During the year 1887, the University of Pennsyl-
vania became a member of the Association, and sent
A. G. Thomson and W. B. Henry to the annual

tournament, which began on the 11th of October at
New Haven. Eleven colleges, a greater number
than ever before, were represented. The most
prominent of the new players were Q. A. Shaw, Jr.,
of Harvard, and O. S. Campbell, of Columbia, both
of whom have since gained distinction in the national
championships at Newport. Knapp had now left
Yale, and that college was represented by Thacher,
Ludington, Shipman and Hurd. Brinley, of Trinity, was the only veteran player who appeared.

The brilliant playing of the Harvard delegation
was the striking feature of the tournament. Harvard
had been unable to make even a fair showing since
the graduation of R. D. Sears, J. S. Clark and H. A.
Taylor, but now her representatives played with
some of the old time skill and captured all of the
honors. P. S. Sears won the Singles championship,
defeating most of the good players, including Weeden
of Brown, Campbell of Columbia, Brinley of Trinity,
and in the final round, the other representative of his
own college, Q. A. Shaw. Jr.

It had been supposed that V. G. Hall and O. S.
Campbell, of Columbia, would win the championship in Doubles, but here again Harvard proved vic-
torious. Sears and Shaw were the winners.

The play in the tournament of the following year,
1888, was almost a repetition of that of 1887. The
same Harvard and Columbia men met in the final
round of Doubles, but Hall and Campbell had now
so improved in skill, that they were able to turn the
tables on Sears and Shaw (7–5. 6-2, 6–3). and add
the inter-collegiate championship to the still greater
honor which they had won earlier in the season,
viz., the Doubles championship of the United

States. In the Singles, Sears repeated his victory of the year before, but only after a most desperate resistance from each of the Columbia players. He defeated Campbell in the semi-finals by a close score (6-3. 5-7. 8-6, 6-4), and in the final and champion-ship round, against V. G. Hall, it became necessary to play the full five sets (7-5, 4-6, 6-2, 4-6. 6-2). Harvard's victory was therefore well earned.

The inter-collegiate tournament of 1889 was some-what disappointing as an exhibition of Lawn Tennis skill, but decidedly interesting in its results. When it became certain that Q. A. Shaw, Jr., of Harvard, would be unable to play, it was generally supposed that O. S. Campbell, of Columbia, who had shortly before made a brilliant record in the All-Comers tournament at Newport, would win an easy victory in the Singles. It was a great surprise, there-fore, when he was defeated by Hovey, of Brown, a clever but not first-class player, in the second round.

With P. S. Sears graduated and Shaw unable to play. Harvard had no chance to win. Her represen-tatives were Messrs. Kingsley and Tallant. After Campbell had been disposed of by Hovey, the cham-pionship became almost a certainty for Yale. It is not often that a Lawn Tennis player, in his very first year of tournament play, is able to make his way into the front ranks and finally end by captur-ing the inter-collegiate championship ; but such was the experience of R. P. Huntington, Jr., of Yale, in 1889. G. A. Hurd, another Yale man, played an exceedingly plucky game, and won the right to contest the final match with Huntington. The two Yale men fought it out, as did Sears and

Shaw of Harvard, in 1887, and Huntington won in straight sets (11-9, 7-5, 6-1).

V. G. Hall had graduated from Columbia, and O. S. Campbell therefore played in the Doubles with A. E. Wright, of the Columbia Law School and formerly of Trinity. This combination was strong enough to win the Doubles championship, though R. P. and F. Huntington, of Yale, gave them a hard fight in the final round (6-4, 6-8, 7-5, 6-4).

The following table gives the complete statistics of the inter-collegiate championships from 1883 to 1889, inclusive:

YEAR.	PLAYED AT	SINGLES.	DOUBLES.	
Spring 1883	Hartford.	J. S. Clark, H.	J. S. Clark, H. A. Taylor,	H.
Fall 1883	Hartford.	H. A. Taylor, H.	H. A. Taylor, P. E. Presbrey,	H.
1884	Hartford.	W. P. Knapp, Y.	W. P. Knapp, W. V. S. Thorne,	Y.
1885	New Haven.	W. P. Knapp, Y.	W. P. Knapp, H. W. Shipman,	Y.
1886	New Haven.	G. M. Brinley, T.	W. P. Knapp, W. L. Thacher,	Y.
1887	New Haven.	P. S. Sears, H.	P. S. Sears, Q A. Shaw, Jr.	H.
1888	New Haven.	P. S. Sears, H.	V. G. Hall, O. S. Campbell,	C.
1889	New Haven.	R.P.Huntington,Jr.,Y.	O. S. Campbell, A. E. Wright,	C.

EVENTS WON.

BY	SINGLES.	DOUBLES.	TOTAL.
Harvard,	4	3	7
Yale, . . .	3	3	6
Columbia, .	0	2	2
Trinity, .	1	0	1

Charles A Chase

CHAPTER VI.

THE SECTIONAL CHAMPIONSHIPS.

MIDDLE STATES—NEW ENGLAND—SOUTHERN STATES—
WESTERN STATES—LONG ISLAND.

THE decision of the sectional championships has been an interesting feature of each season's play. The idea originated in the year 1885, when the St. George's Cricket Club, of New York, applied to the United States National Lawn Tennis Association for the right to hold a tournament, under the auspices of the Association, for the championship of the Middle States. The requisite authority having been given, the first meeting was held on the grounds of the St. George's Cricket Club, at Hoboken, N. J., early in the month of June, 1885. It resulted in Mr. R. D. Sears being declared the champion of the Middle States. The following table is a complete record of the championships of this section.

MIDDLE STATES.

YEAR	CHAMPION.	WINNER OF TOURNAMENT.	DOUBLES CHAMPIONS.
1885	R. D. Sears.	R. D. Sears.	R. D. Sears & J. S. Clark.
1886	R. L. Beeckman.	R. L. Beeckman.	R.L. Beeckman & H.W. Slocum, Jr.
1887	R. L. Beeckman.	R. L. Beeckman.	
1888	E. P. McMullen.	E. P. McMullen.	
1889	H. A. Taylor.	H. A. Taylor.	

In the following year, 1886, the New Haven
Lawn Club held a tournament, also under the auspices of the Association, for the championship of
New England. The same club has since continued to give this tournament, as an annual event.

NEW ENGLAND.

YEAR	CHAMPION.	WINNER OF TOURNAMENT.	DOUBLES CHAMPIONS.
1886	H.W. Slocum, Jr.	H. W. Slocum, Jr.	H. W. Slocum, Jr. W. L. Thacher.
1887	H.W. Slocum, Jr.	H. W. Slocum, Jr.	F.G.Beach & W. L. Thacher.
1888	H.W. Slocum, Jr.	E. P. McMullen.	V. G. Hall & O. S. Campbell
1889	H.W. Slocum, Jr.	R. P. Huntington, Jr.	F. G. Beach, R. P. Huntington, Jr.

The tournaments for the championship of the
South have been played in various cities, including
Wilmington, Baltimore and Washington. In 1887
and the spring of 1888, the meetings in the South
were not held under the auspices of the National
Association, but the results are given in the following table, so that the record may not be incomplete.

SOUTHERN STATES.

YEAR.	PLAYED AT	SINGLES CHAMPION.	DOUBLES CHAMPIONS.
1886	Wilmington.	C. B. Davis.	C. B. Davis & R. H. F. Porter.
1887	Washington.	Leigh Bonsal.	L. Bonsal & L. V. Lemoyne.
Spring 1888	Baltimore.	A. H. S. Post.	L. Bonsal & L. V. Lemoyne.
Fall 1888	Washington.	F. Mansfield.	F. Mansfield & F. L.V. Hoppin.
1889	Washington.	F. Mansfield.	C. J. Post & M. F. Prosser.

In 1887 the Chicago Tennis Club, of Chicago, Ill., held the first tournament for the championship of the West. Mr. C. A. Chase, of Chicago, is by far the best player which the West has produced. He has held the title of champion from 1887 up to the present time.

WESTERN STATES.

YEAR.	CHAMPION.	WINNER OF TOURNAMENT.	DOUBLES CHAMPIONS.
1887	C. A. Chase.	C. A. Chase.	E. B. McClellan & B. F. Cummins.
1888	C. A. Chase.	E. B. McClellan.	E. B. McClellan & B. F. Cummins.
1889	C. A. Chase.	S. T. Chase.	C. A. Chase & S. T. Chase.

The following is a record of the championships of Long Island, which have been decided annually upon the grounds of the Meadow Club of Southampton.

LONG ISLAND.

YEAR	CHAMPION.	WINNER OF TOURNAMENT.	DOUBLES CHAMPIONS.
1887	H. A. Taylor.	H. A. Taylor.	H. A. Taylor & H. W. Slocum, Jr.
1888	H. A. Taylor.	J. S. Clark.	F. Keene & H. W. Slocum, Jr.
1889	H. A. Taylor.	J. S. Clark.	F. Keene & H. A. Taylor.

APPENDIX.

LAWS OF LAWN TENNIS.

As Adopted, Revised and Amended by the United States
National Lawn Tennis Association, at Annual
Conventions, 1881–90.

THE COURT.

1. **The Court** is 78 feet long, and 27 feet wide. It is divided across the middle by a net, the ends of which are attached to two posts, **A** and **B**, standing 3 feet outside of

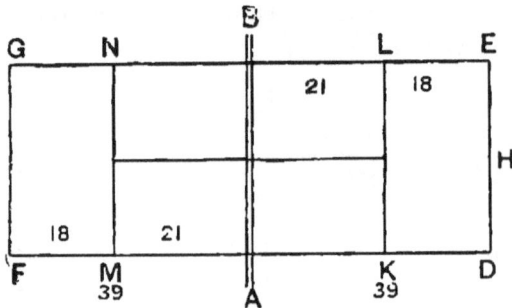

the court on either side. The height of the net is 3 feet 6 inches at the posts, and 3 feet in the middle. At each end of the court, parallel with the net, and 39 feet from it, are drawn the base lines **DE** and **FG**, the ends of which are connected by the side-lines **DF** and **EG**. Half way between side lines, and parallel with them, is drawn the half court line **IH**, dividing the space on each side of the net into two equal parts, the right and left courts. On each side of the net, at a distance of 21 feet from it, and parallel with it, are drawn the service lines **KL** and **MN**.

THE BALLS.

2. **The Balls** shall measure not less than $2\frac{15}{32}$ inches, nor more than 2½ inches in diameter ; and shall weigh not less than $1\frac{15}{16}$ oz., nor more than 2 oz.

THE GAME.

3. The choice of sides, and the right to serve in the first game, shall be decided by toss ; provided that, if the winner of the toss choose the right to serve, the other player shall have choice of sides, and vice versa. If one player choose the court, the other may elect not to serve.

4. The players shall stand on opposite sides of the net ; the player who first delivers the ball shall be called the server, and the other the striker-out.

5. At the end of the first game the striker-out shall become server, and the server shall become striker-out ; and so on alternately in all the subsequent games of the set, or series of sets.

6. **The Server** shall serve with one foot on the base line or perpendicularly above said line, and with the other foot behind said line, but not necessarily upon the ground. He shall deliver the service from the right to left courts, alternately, beginning from the right.

7. The ball served must drop between the service line, half court line, and side line of the court, diagonally opposite to that from which it was served.

8. It is a **Fault** in the server fail to strike the ball, or if the ball served drop in the net, or beyond the service line, or out of court, or in the wrong court ; or if the server do not stand as directed by law 6.

9. A ball falling on a line is regarded as falling in the court bounded by that line.

10. A fault cannot be taken.

11. After a fault the server shall serve again from the same court from which he served that fault, unless it was a fault because he served from the wrong court.

12. A fault cannot be claimed after the next service is delivered.

13. The server shall not serve till the striker-out is ready. If the latter attempt to return the service he shall be deemed ready.

14. A service or fault delivered when the striker-out is not ready, counts for nothing.

15. The service shall not be volleyed, *i. e.*, taken, before it has touched the ground.

16. A ball is in play on leaving the server's racket, except as provided for in law 8.

17. It is a good return, although the ball touch the net; but a service, otherwise good, which touches the net, shall count for nothing.

18. The server wins a stroke if the striker-out volley the service, or if he fail to return the service or the ball in play; or if he return the service or the ball in play so that it drops outside of his opponent's court; or if he otherwise lose a stroke, as provided by law 20.

19. The striker-out wins a stroke if the server serve two consecutive faults; or if he fail to return the ball in play; or if he return the ball in play so that it drops outside of his opponent's court; or if he otherwise lose a stroke, as provided by law 20.

20. Either player loses a stroke if the ball touch him, or anything that he wears or carries, except his racquet in the act of striking; or if he touch the ball with his racquet more than once; or if he touch the net or any of its supports while the ball is in play; or if he volley the ball before it has passed the net.

21. In case any player is obstructed by any accident, the ball shall be considered a let.

22. On either player winning his first stroke, the score is called 15 for that player; on either player winning his second stroke, the score is called 30 for that player; on either player winning his third stroke, the stroke is called 40 for that player; and the fourth stroke won by either player

is scored game for that player, except as below: If both players have won three strokes, the score is called *deuce ;* and the net stroke won by either player is scored *advantage* for that player. If the same player wins the next stroke, he wins the game; if he loses the next stroke the score returns to deuce; and so on until one player wins the two strokes immediately following the score of deuce, when game is scored for that player.

23. The player who first wins six games, wins the set; except as below: If both players win five games, the score is called *games all;* and the next game won by either player is scored *advantage game* for that player. If the same player wins the next game he wins the set; if he loses the next game, the score returns to games all; and so on, until either player wins the two games immediately following the score of games all, when he wins the set. But individual clubs, at their own tournaments, may modify this rule at their discretion.

24. The players shall change sides at the end of every set; but the umpire, on appeal from either player, before the toss for choice, shall direct the players to change sides at the end of the first, third, fifth and every alternate game succeeding thereafter in each set, if, in his opinion, either side have a distinct advantage, owing to the sun, wind, or any other accidental cause; but if the appeal be made after the toss for choice, the umpire can only direct the players to change sides at the end of the first, third, fifth and every alternate game succeeding thereafter in the odd or deciding set.

25. When a series of sets is played, the player who served in the last game of one set shall be striker-out in the first game of the next.

26. In all contests the play shall be continuous from the first service till the match be concluded, but upon application by either player for reason or reasons which may seem adequate to the referee, an interval, which shall not exceed two minutes, may be allowed between successive rests. If the interval be between successive sets, seven minutes may be allowed. The referee at his discretion may at any time

postpone the match on account of rain or darkness, or may otherwise waive the provisions of this rule, on the expressed consent of both players. In any case of postponement the previous score shall hold good. Where play has ceased for more than an hour, the player, who at the cessation thereof was on the side of the net originally first chosen, shall have the choice of sides on the recommencement of play. He will stay on the side he chooses for the remainder of the set, and then alternate each subsequent set.

The last two sentences of this rule do not apply when the players are changing every game.

27. The above laws shall apply to the three-handed and four-handed games, except as below :—

THE THREE-HANDED AND FOUR-HANDED GAMES.

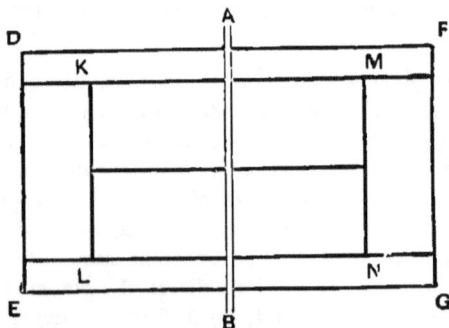

28. For the three-handed and four-handed games the court shall be 36 feet in width; 4½ feet inside the side lines, and parallel with them are drawn the service side lines KM and LN. The service lines are not drawn beyond the point at which they meet the service side lines, as shown in the diagram.

29. In the three-handed game, the single player shall serve in every alternate game.

30. In the four-handed game, the pair who have the right to serve in the first game shall decide which partner

shall do so; and the opposing pair shall decide in like manner for the second game. The partner of the player who served in the first game shall serve in the third, and the partner of the player who served in the second game shall serve in the fourth, and the same order shall be maintained in all the subsequent games of the set.

31. At the beginning of the next set either partner of the pair which struck out in the last game of the last set may serve; and the same privilege is given to their opponents in second game of the new set.

32. The players shall take the service alternately throughout the game ; a player cannot receive a service delivered to his partner; and the order of service and striking out once established shall not be altered, nor shall the striker-out change courts to receive the service, till the end of the set.

33. If a player serve out of his turn, the umpire, as soon as the mistake is discovered by himself or one of the players, shall direct the player to serve who ought to have served. But all strokes scored and any faults served before such discovery, shall be reckoned. If a game shall be completed before such discovery, then the service in the next alternate game shall be delivered by the partner of the player who served out of his turn, and so on in regular rotation.

34. It is a fault if the ball served does not drop between the service-line, half-court line, and service side line of the court, diagonally opposite to that from which it was served.

35. It is a fault if the ball served does not drop as provided in law 34, or if it touches the server's partner or anything he wears or carries.

36. In matches, the decision of the umpire shall be final. Should there be two umpires, they shall divide the court between them, and the decision of each shall be final in his share of the court.

ODDS.

37. **A Bisque** is one point which can be taken by the receiver of the odds at any time in the set, except as follows :

(*a.*) A bisque cannot be taken after a service is delivered.

(*b.*) The server may not take a bisque after a fault, but the striker-out may do so.

38. One or more bisques may be given to increase or diminish other odds.

39. Half fifteen is one stroke given at the beginning of the second, fourth, and every subsequent alternate game of a set

40. Fifteen is one stroke given at the beginning of every game of a set.

41. Half thirty is one stroke given at the beginning of the first game, two strokes given at the beginning of the second game, and so on alternately in all the subsequent games of the set.

42. Thirty is two strokes given at the beginning of every game of the set.

43. Half forty is two strokes given at the beginning of the first game, three strokes given at the beginning of the second game, and so on alternately in all the subsequent games of the set.

44. Forty is three strokes given at the beginning of every game of a set.

45. Half Court: the players may agree into which half court, right or left, the giver of the odds shall play ; and the latter loses a stroke if the ball returned by him drops outside any of the lines which bound that half court.

46. Owed odds are where the giver of the odds starts behind scratch.

47. Owe half fifteen is one stroke owed at the beginning of the first, third, and every subsequent alternate game of a set.

48. Owe fifteen is one stroke owed at the beginning of every game of a set.

49. Owe half thirty is two strokes owed at the beginning of the first game, one stroke owed at the beginning of the second game, and so on alternately through all the subsequent games of the set.

50. Owe thirty is two strokes owed at the beginning of every game of a set.

51. Owe half forty is three strokes owed at the beginning of the first game, two strokes owed at the beginning of the second game, and so on alternately in all subsequent games of the set.

52. Owe forty is three strokes owed at the beginning of every game of a set.

OFFICERS AND MEMBERS

OF THE

UNITED STATES

NATIONAL LAWN TENNIS ASSOCIATION.

(APRIL, 1890.)

——:o:——

OFFICERS OF THE ASSOCIATION.

PRESIDENT.

JOSEPH S. CLARK, . . . Young America Cricket Club
139 South Fourth Street, Philadelphia, Pa.

VICE-PRESIDENT.

H. W. SLOCUM, JR. . . . St. George's Cricket Club
Garfield Building, Brooklyn, N. Y.

SECRETARY.

VALENTINE G. HALL, . Edgewood Lawn Tennis Club
11 West 37th Street, N. Y. City.

TREASURER.

HOWARD A. TAYLOR, . Country Club of Westchester County
280 Broadway, N. Y. City.

EXECUTIVE COMMITTEE.

R. D. SEARS, JAMES DWIGHT, JOSEPH WHITTLESEY.
F. H. OUTERBRIDGE, C. E. STICKNEY

MEMBERS OF THE ASSOCIATION.

CLASS I.

Belmont Cricket Club—MILTON C. WORK, Secretary, Girard Building, Philadelphia, Pa.

Bergen Point Athletic Club—MRS..A. C. STEVENS, Secretary, 201 W. 103d St., New York City.

Berkeley Athletic Club—J. CLARK READ, Secretary, 19 W. 44th St., New York City.

Bridgeport Lawn Tennis Club—FRANK SLASON, Secretary, 354 Main St., Bridgeport, Conn.

Brooklyn Heights Tennis Club—F. J. PHILLIPS, Secretary, 98 Joralemon St., Brooklyn, N. Y.

Brooklyn Hill Tennis Club—REMSON JOHNSON, Secretary, 168 Hancock St., Brooklyn, N. Y.

Buffalo Tennis Club—E. P. COTTLE, Secretary, 424 Main St., Buffalo, N. Y.

California Lawn Tennis Club—E. N. BEE, Secretary, 208 California St., San Francisco, Cal.

Cheyenne Lawn Tennis Club—LOCKWOOD HEBARD, Secretary, Cheyenne, Wyoming.

Chicago Tennis Club—E. M. SKINNER, Secretary, care of Marshall Field & Co. (Wholesale), Chicago, Ill.

Chestnut Hill Lawn Tennis Club—MISS RUTH COIT, Secretary, Chestnut Hill, Philadelphia, Pa.

Clifton Tennis and Base Ball Club—MISS ANNA T. RIPLEY, Secretary, Rose Bank P. O., Staten Island.

Columbia College L. T. Association—O. S. CAMPBELL, Secretary, 18 Remsen St., Brooklyn, N. Y.

Colorado Springs Lawn Tennis Club—G. A. MACKLIN, Secretary, P. O. Box 44, Colorado Springs, Col.

Country Club of Westchester Co.—E. HAIGHT, Secretary, 26 Broad St., New York City.

Country Club of Maryland—F. P. MacLean, Secretary, 1519 Rhode Island Ave., Washington, D. C.

Crescent Club of Mt. Vernon—H. M. Williams, Secretary, 15 Cortlandt St., New York City.

Danbury Lawn Tennis Club—Granville Whittlesey, Secretary, Danbury, Conn.

Dayton Lawn Tennis Club—T. E. Van Ansdal, Secretary, 23 South Main St., Dayton, Ohio.

Delaware Field Club—E. H. Gayley, Secretary, 7th and Market Sts., Wilmington, Del.

East Orange Lawn Tennis and Athletic Assciation—Robert Slimmon, Secretary, 12 College Place, New York City.

Edgewood Club of Tivoli-on-Hudson—C. L. Clarkson, Secretary, 55 Liberty St., New York City.

Elmwood Lawn Tennis Club—W. H. Wing, Secretary, 10 South Water St., Providence, R. I.

Englewood Field Club—Edgar H Booth, Secretary, 11 Wall St., N. Y. City.

Flushing Athletic Club—Henry K. Gilman, Secretary, Flushing, Long Island.

Germantown Cricket Club—F. M. Bissell, Secretary, 243 South Fourth St , Philadelphia, Pa.

Harvard University L. T. Association—Hugh Tallant, Secretary, 9 Holyoke House, Cambridge, Mass.

Hohokus Valley Tennis Club—Stephen W. Orne, Secretary, Ridgewood, N. J.

Kenwood Lawn Tennis Club—Henry M. Lane, Secretary, 286 48th St., Chicago, Ill.

Lenox Club—Hamilton Kuhn, Secretary, Lenox, Mass.

Litchfield Lawn Club — F. S. Woodruff, Secretary, Litchfield, Conn.

Longwood Cricket Club—Lott Mansfield, Secretary, 280 Darmouth St., Boston, Mass.

Luzerne Club—Ogle T. Warren, Secretary, 19 Second St., Troy, N. Y.

Meadow Club of South Hampton—E. W. Humphreys, Secretary, 54 Exchange Place, New York City.

Merion Cricket Club—Edward S. Sayres, Secretary, 217 South Third St., Philadelphia, Pa.

Minnesota Lawn Tennis Club—J. M. Blakeley, Secretary, Gilfillan Block, St. Paul, Minn.

Montclair Tennis Club—James S. Poeter, Secretary, Montclair, N. J.

Morristown Lawn Tennis Club—GILBERT P. BULLOCK, Secretary, Morristown, N. J.

Murray Hill Tennis Club—L. WATER LIMAN, Secretary, 66 Leonard St., New York City.

Narragansett Lawn Tennis Club—LLOYD SALTUS, Secretary, Narragansett Casino, R. I.

New Haven Lawn Club—DR. W. G. DAGGETT, Secretary, Cor. College and Crown Sts., New Haven, Conn.

New Hamburgh Lawn Tennis Club—C. R. SANDS, Secreretary, 385 5th Ave., New York City.

Newport Tennis Club—W. WATTS SHERMAN, Secretary, Newport, R. I.

New York Tennis Club—CLARENCE HOBART, Secretary, 731 St. Nicholas Ave., New York City.

New York Athletic Club—F. D. STURGIS, Secretary, 104 West 55th St., New York City.

North End Tennis Club—L. V. LEMOYNE, Treasurer, 121 La Salle St., Chicago, Ill.

North Shore Tennis Club—W. Y. WEMPLE, Secretary, New Brighton, Staten Island.

Nutley Field Club—H. G. PROUT, Secretary, 73 Broadway, New York City.

Orange Lawn Tennis Club—S. M. Colgate, Secretary, 55 John St., New York City.

Orange Athletic Club—W. O. WILEY, Secretary, 15 Halstead St., East Orange, N. J.

Passaic Lawn Tennis Club—F. A. MARSELLUS, Secretary, Passaic, N. J.

Philadelphia Cricket Club—ALAN H. HARRIS, Secretary, 116 South 3d St., Philadelphia, Pa.

Pittsburg Cricket Club—CHARLES S. CLARK, Secretary, Penn and Dallas Ave., Pittsburg, Pa.

Portland Lawn Tennis Club—S. C. FOX, Secretary, 121 Emery St., Portland, Maine.

Ridgefield Athletic Club—WILLIAM BRUCE, Secretary, New York State National Bank, Albany, N. Y.

Rochester Tennis Club—W. J. CURTIS, Secretary, Union and Advertiser Co., Rochester, N. Y.

Rockaway Hunting Club—MIDDLETON S. BURRILL, Secretary, 21 Broad St., Mills Building, New York City.

Scarsdale Lawn Tennis Club—C. C. FLEMING, Secretary, Second National Bank, 190 5th Ave., New York City.

Seabright Lawn Tennis and Cricket Club—F. J. ALLIEN, Secretary, 1 Broadway, New York City.

Springfield Tennis Ccmpa¬y—H. G. CHAPIN, Secretary,
Springfield, Mass.

St. Augustine Tennis Club—G. S. SMITH, Secretary, 536
5th Ave., New York City.

Staten Island Cricket and Baseball Club—R. ST. GEORGE
WALKER, Secretary, 53 Beaver St., New York City.

Staten Island Ladies' Club—MRS GEO. L. UPSHUR, Secretary, New Brighton, Staten Island.

St. George's Cricket Club—W. E. GLYN, Secretary, 30
Broad St., New York City.

Summit Lawn Tennis Club—W. Y. HAWKS, Secretary,
Summit, N. J.

Taunton Tennis Association—ALBERT FULLER, Secretary,
Taunton, Mass.

Tioga Athletic Association—JOSEPH T. SILL, Secretary, 329
Chestnut St., Philadelphia, Pa.

Trinity College Lawn Tennis Club—T. A. CONOVER, Secretary, Trinity College, Hartford, Conn.

Twenty-third Regiment Tennis Club—J. W. RAYMOND,
Secretary, 7 Wall St., New York City.

Tuxedo Club—WILLIAM KENT, Secretary, 59 Liberty St.,
New York City.

Waterbury Lawn Tennis Club—C. E. MUNGER, Secretary,
Waterbury, Conn.

Wedgmere Tennis Club—C. H. TYLER, Secretary, Winchester, Mass.

West End Iawn Tennis Club—HENRY C. SNOW, President, 27 Newberry St., Boston, Mass.

Yale University Lawn Tennis Association—C. P. HOWLAND,
Secretary, 156 Farnam St., New Haven, Conn.

Young America Cricket Club—I. R. DAVIS, Secretary, 257
South Fourth St., Philadelphia, Pa.

CLASS II.

Hudson River Lawn Tennis Association—DR. W. G. MURDOCK, Secretary, Cold Springs-on-the-Hudson, N. Y.

ALL ENGLAND CHAMPIONSHIPS.

SINGLES.

YEAR.	CHAMPION.	ALL-COMERS, WINNER.	RUNNER-UP.
1877	S. W. Gore.	S. W. Gore.	W. Marshall.
1878	P. F. Hadow.	P. F. Hadow.	W. Erskine.
1879	J. T. Hartley.	J. T. Hartle .	V. St. Ledger.
1880	J. T. Hartley.	H. F. Lawford.	O. E. Woodhouse.
1881	W. Renshaw.	W. Renshaw.	R. T. Richardson.
1882	W. Renshaw.	E. Renshaw.	R. T. Richardson.
1883	W. Renshaw.	E. Renshaw.	Donald Stewart.
1884	W. Renshaw.	H. F. Lawford.	C. W. Grinstead.
1885	W. Renshaw.	H. F. Lawford.	E. Renshaw.
1886	W. Renshaw.	H. F. Lawford.	E. W. Lewis.
1887	H. F. Lawford.	H. F. Lawford.	E. Renshaw.
1888	E. Renshaw.	E. Renshaw.	E. W. Lewis.
1889	W. Renshaw.	W. Renshaw.	H. S. Barlow.

DOUBLES.

YEAR	CHAMPIONS.	RUNNERS-UP.
1879	L. K. Erskine & H. F. Lawford.	F. Durant & G. E. Tabor.
1880	W. Renshaw & E. Renshaw.	O. E. Woodhouse & C. J. Cole.
1881	W. Renshaw & E. Renshaw.	W. J. Down & H. Vaughan.
1882	J. T. Hartley & R. T. Richardson.	J. G. Horn & C. B. Russell.
1883	C. W. Grinstead & C. E. Welldon.	C. B. Russell & R. T. Milford.
1884	W. Renshaw & E. Renshaw.	E. L. Williams & E. W. Lewis.
1885	W. Renshaw & E. Renshaw.	A. J. Stanley & C. E. Farrer.
1886	W. Renshaw & E. Renshaw.	A. J. Stanley & C. E. Farrer.
1887	Hon.P.B.Lyon &H.W.Wilberforce.	J. H. Crispe & E. Barratt-Smith.
1888	W. Renshaw & E. Renshaw.	E. G. Meers & A. G. Ziffo.
1889	W. Renshaw & E. Renshaw.	E. W. Lewis & G. W. Hillyard.

RULES FOR HANDICAPPING.

When two players, both in receipt of odds, meet, the player receiving the smaller odds is put back to scratch. The following table shows the point at which the other should then start. The number at the left of the horizontal columns denotes the player who goes back to scratch, those at the head of the vertical columns the player who still receives odds; and the numbers within the columns show the odds to be received by the player whose number stands at the head of the column.

No.	1	2	3	4	5	6	7	8	9	10	11	12	13	14	15
1 (I bis.)		2 bis.	Half-15	Half-15 & I bis.	Half-15 & 2 bis.	15	15 and I bis.	15 and 2 bis.	Half-30	Half-30 & I bis.	Half-30 & 2 bis.	30	30 and I bis.	30 and 2 bis.	Half-40
2 (2 bis.)			2 bis.	Half-15	Half-15 & I bis.	Half-15 & 2 bis.	15	15 and I bis.	15 and 2 bis.	Half-30	Half-30 & I bis.	Half-30 & 2 bis.	30	30 and I bis.	30 and 2 bis.
3 (Half-15)				2 bis.	Half-15	Half-15 & I bis.	Half-15 & 2 bis.	15	15 and I bis.	15 and 2 bis.	Half-30	Half-30 & I bis.	Half-30 & 2 bis.	30	30 and I bis.
4 (Half-15 & I bis.)					2 bis.	Half-15	Half-15 & I bis.	Half-15 & 2 bis.	15	15 and I bis.	15 and 2 bis.	Half-30	Half-30 & I bis.	Half-30 & 2 bis.	30
5 (Half-15 & 2 bis.)						2 bis.	Half-15	Half-15 & I bis.	Half-15 & 2 bis.	15	15 and I bis.	15 and 2 bis.	Half-30	Half-30 & I bis.	Half-30 & 2 bis.
6 (15)							2 bis.	Half-15	Half-15 & I bis.	Half-15 & 2 bis.	15	15 and I bis.	15 and 2 bis.	Half-30	Half-30 & I bis.
7 (15 and I bis.)								2 bis.	Half-15	Half-15 & I bis.	Half-15 & 2 bis.	15	15 and I bis.	15 and 2 bis.	Half-30
8 (15 and 2 bis.)									2 bis.	Half-15	Half-15 & I bis.	Half-15 & 2 bis.	15	15 and I bis.	15 and 2 bis.
9 (Half-30)										2 bis.	Half-15	Half-15 & I bis.	Half-15 & 2 bis.	15	15 and I bis.
10 (Half-30 & I bis.)											2 bis.	Half-15	Half-15 & I bis.	Half-15 & 2 bis.	15
11 (Half-30 & 2 bis.)												2 bis.	Half-15	Half-15 & I bis.	Half-15 & 2 bis.
12 (30)													2 bis.	Half-15	Half-15 & I bis.
13 (30 and I bis.)														2 bis.	Half-15
14 (30 and 2 bis.)															2 bis.

When two players meet who are handicapped to *owe* odds, the player owing the lesser odds is placed at scratch. This table shows the odds the other will still owe:

	1	2	3	4	5	6	7	8	9	10	11	12
1	1	Half-15 for 1 bis	Half-15	15 for 2 bis.	15 for 1 bis.	15	Half-30 for 2 bis	Half-30 for 1 bis	Half-30	30 for 2 bis.	30 for 1 bis.	30
2		2	Half-15 for 1 bis	Half-15	15 for 2 bis.	15 for 1 bis.	15	Half-30 for 2 bis	Half-30 for 1 bis	Half-30	30 for 2 bis.	30 for 1 bis.
3			3	Half-15 for 1 bis	Half-15	15 for 2 bis.	15 for 1 bis.	15	Half-30 for 2 bis	Half-30 for 1 bis	Half-30 for 1 bis	Half-30
4				4	Half-15 for 1 bis	Half-15	15 for 2 bis.	15 for 1 bis.	15	Half-30 for 2 bis	Half-30 for 2 bis	Half-30 for 1 bis
5					5	Half-15 for 1 bis	Half-15	15 for 2 bis.	15 for 1 bis.	15	15	Half-30 for 2 bis
6						6	Half-15 for 1 bis	Half-15	15 for 2 bis.	15 for 1 bis.	15 for 1 bis.	15
7							7	Half-15 for 1 bis	Half-15	15 for 2 bis.	15 for 2 bis.	15 for 1 bis.
8								8	Half-15 for 1 bis	Half-15	Half-15	15 for 2 bis.
9									9	Half-15 for 1 bis	Half-15 for 1 bis	Half-15
10										10	Half-15 for 2 bis	Half-15 for 1 bis
11											11	Half-15 for 2 bis

THE BAGNALL-WILD SYSTEM OF DRAWING.*

The object of this method of drawing is to eliminate all the byes in the first round, both for convenience and still more because a bye is of less value in the first round than later in the tournament.

If the number of entries is a power of 2, e. g., 4, 8, 16, 32, or 64, there need be no byes. In other cases a preliminary round must be played, in which there shall be as many matches as the number of entries exceeds the power of 2 next below, all the other contestants having byes.

For example, suppose that there are 37 entries. The power of 2 next below is 32, therefore there must be 5 matches and 27 byes.

In this way the five losers go out and the number of contestants is reduced to 32, which will always divide by 2 (16, 8, 4, 2, 1).

The names should be written on slips of paper and the slips carefully folded and put in a hat. They are then drawn one by one and written one below the other, the pairs that are to play together being bracketed. One-half the byes should come first, next the matches, last the remaining byes. Should there be an uneven number of byes, the odd one goes at the bottom. One example will suffice. There are 19 entries; three matches must be played to reduce the number to 16; that will leave 13 byes, 6 at the top of the list and 7 at the bottom, as follows:

SECOND ROUND.

P takes first prize; G second; D and O equal thirds.

JAMES DWIGHT.

*Reprinted by permission from Wright & Ditson, of Boston, Mass